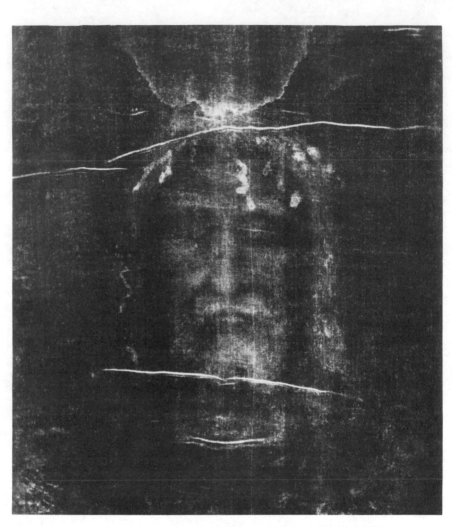

THE FACE OF JESUS

*Accurately produced from the impression
on his burial shroud*

The
GLORY OF THY PEOPLE

THE STORY OF A CONVERSION

RAPHAEL SIMON, O.C.S.O.

Monk of the Order of Cistercians of the Strict Observance (Trappists)
St. Joseph's Abbey

With Preface by

Most Reverend Fulton J. Sheen, D.D.

St. Bede's Publications
Petersham, Massachusetts

Nihil Obstat   Fr. M. Alberic Wulf, OCSO
                Fr. M. Gabriel O'Connell, OCSO
                                       Censors
November 25, 1946

Imprimatur   Fr. M. Dominique Nogues
              Abbot General of the Order of Cistercians
              of the Strict Observance
April 19, 1947

Nihil Obstat   Thomas C. Collins
                Censor Librorum

Imprimatur   +Francis P. Keough
              Bishop of Providence
Providence, Rhode Island
April 9, 1947

For Revised Edition

Imprimatur   +Timothy J. Harrington
              Bishop of Worcester, Massachusetts
February 25, 1986

The Nihil Obstat and Imprimatur are official declarations that a book is considered to be free of doctrinal and moral error. It is not implied that those who have granted the Nihil Obstat and Imprimatur necessarily agree with the contents, opinions or statements expressed.

LIBRARY OF CONGRESS CATALOGING IN PUBLICATION DATA

Simon, Raphael.
  The glory of thy people.

  1. Simon, Raphael.   2. Converts, Catholic—United States—Biography.
3. Converts from Judaism—Biography.   I. Title.
BX4668.S5A34   1986   248.2'46'0924   [B]   86-3836
ISBN 0-932506-47-X

I DEDICATE THIS LITTLE BOOK

TO ST. BERNARD, CISTERCIAN ABBOT,

Father of contemplatives and Protector of Jews.

" . . . touch not the Hebrews. Speak to them with kindness, for they are of the flesh and bone of the Messiah: to harm them is to wound the Saviour in the apple of His eye." Thus spoke this wise man, and his voice prevailed, because he was loved and revered by all. It was his heart that led him to love them (the Jews) and prompted him to speak good words for Israel.—*Joshua Ben-Meir, a Jewish writer and contemporary, with reference to St. Bernard's defense of the Jews in the time of a persecution.*

CONTENTS

ACKNOWLEDGMENTS

To Miss Rosalie Marie Levy, Catholic, Jewish convert and author. It was in compliance with her request for the story of my conversion—which reached my Novice Master in the days of my novitiate that these pages were written. From them she prepared an abstract which appeared in her autobiography *Thirty Years with Christ*.

To Charles Rich, Jewish convert, my companion in Christ, who "discovered" this manuscript about two years after it was written, and after having solicited the opinions of literary judges, urged its publication.

To the late Reverend Ignatius Cox, s.j., of Fordham University, whose recommendations and encouragement brought about the publication of this book.

To the Very Reverend Timothy M. Sparks, o.p., s.t.d., to whose counsel, prayers and example I owe my progress in the spiritual life from the time of my baptism until that of my entrance into the monastery, and to whom I am indebted for correction of the original manuscript.

To the late Right Reverend Dom M. Edmund Futterer, o.c.s.o., Abbot of Our Lady of the Valley and founding Abbot of St. Joseph's Abbey, who authorized the original publication of this book.

To the late Dr. Herbert Schwartz, who typed the original manuscript.

Sincere thanks to Houghton Mifflin Company for permission to print an excerpt from *Report on the Shroud of Turin* by John Heller. Copyright 1983 by John H. Heller.

To America Press, Inc. 106 West 56 St., New York, NY 10019 for permission to quote from *The Documents of Vatican II*, Abbott-Gallagher edition, Copyright 1966. All Rights Reserved.

And to America Press, Inc. and to John Tracy Ellis for permission to reprint an excerpt on "Catholic Intellectual Life: 1984" from the 10-6-84 issue of *America*. Copyright 1984. All Rights Reserved.

To Professor Ferdynand Zweig and Heinemann Educational Books, 22 Bedford Square, London for permission to quote from *Israel: The Sword and the Harp*.

PREFACE

This is the spiritual Odyssey of a soul—a story which most intrigues men in these dark days, when the promised progress of the nineteenth century collapsed into the despair of the twentieth. It is very interesting that practically no one ever writes the story of his conversion into any sect, but only when he comes into the Catholic Church. This is because one generally remains on the human level until lifted into the supernatural order where truth is more than human, sacraments more than subjective, and religion more than a high form of sociability. But even when the convert becomes a Catholic, the story must necessarily be incomplete, for even the more detailed record of conversion's antecedents, and the most elaborate reasons for a change of heart, leave out the action of Divine Grace in the human soul, and the cooperation of the human will. As Our Blessed Lord told Peter when He made his confession of Divinity: "Flesh and blood hath not revealed it to thee, but My Father Who is in Heaven."

Particularly interesting is this record of spiritual growth, for two reasons: it comes from the pen of a scientist and a Jew, and ends with the scientist becoming more scientific than ever, and the Jew still more of a Jew. As a scientist, a doctor of medicine, and a psychiatrist, the author saw that no science was complete which counted the letters and the words in the book of Nature, but never inquired either who wrote the book, or the moral obligations of him who studied it. Psychiatry is a modern science, and its success is in large part due to the fact that it plays on the fringes of the great historical fact of original sin. The tensions, the dialectic, the conflicts within the human soul are discovered in most cases to be due not to the pressure of moral inhibitions, but to an unrequited sense of guilt. The author has come to see that

ix

what human souls need for peace is less sublimation than an absolution, less the need of having sin explained away and more the need of having sins forgiven. In this sense, his conversion is not so much the story of a man turning his back on the scientific and the psychologic as that of finding in religion their complement and perfection.

The same is true of his Jewish background which he sees as perfected in the faith. To him who ought to know, the relation between the Jew and the Christian is the relation of father to son, roots to branches, which is confirmed in the words of the Canon of the Mass: *The sacrifice of Abraham, our father in faith.* Though few Jews and Christians realize the full import of this idea which is so beautifully portrayed by the author, the fact remains that major catastrophes of our times have witnessed both the persecution of the Old Testament by the Nazis and the persecution of the New Testament by the Communists. Some great demonic force has been let loose in the world which hates both those who gave Christ to the world and those who follow Him. The demonic spirit that hates both Jew and Christian is a revelation that both are "outsiders" to its spirit, and that neither the finger of Abraham nor the finger of Christ will be welcome into the city of man. The fact that Jew and Christian are being persecuted together, is not only a proof that the anti-God spirit of the world persecutes all who have had any vocational dealings with God, but it also augurs for the future day when the two, who are hated by a common enemy, will be driven into one another's arms. Neither the Jew nor the Christian, however faithless either is to his faith, will ever be absorbed by the world, for they are a ferment and nonassimilative group who will find rest neither in a secularized Messianism, nor a humanism without Christ, but only in the fulfillment of the supernal vocation to which they have been called.

In the small compass of this story the mystical truth stands out that to persecute the house of Israel is to persecute not the Mystical Body of Christ, but its fleshy lineage, and that in the passion of Israel in the world, Christ suffers as the

Shepherd of Sion, the Messiah of Israel. The darkness of the present day may be but a preparation for that blessed day when, in the language of St. Thomas Aquinas, the Jews "will call back life to the Gentiles, the lukewarm faithful, whose charity because of the growth of iniquity, will have grown cold." This spiritual autobiography of Father M. Raphael Simon[1] is that hope in miniature.

Those who read his story may quarrel with the reasons he alleges, and may think they find a flaw in his logic, but let those who so find fault ask themselves if what they believe is believed with the same conviction as this man's, who left a promising career to prove the truth of his conviction by becoming a monk in one of the strictest orders of the Church. Here is a man who went the whole way, who was content with no half-drawn swords, divided loyalties and compromising surrenders. Pascal once said in defense of the Evangelists' writing the truth in their Gospels: "I will believe any man who has his throat cut for a cause." And here, without saying it, the reader will be faced with one unanswerable argument: I will believe any man who leaves what Dr. Simon left to become a Monk of the Order of the Cistercians of the Strict Observance, and to live the rest of his days in the shades and shadows of the Cross where Saints are made.

Archbishop Fulton J. Sheen

---

[1] Doctor Alwyn Kenneth Simon is known in religion as Father Raphael, O.C.S.O.

INTRODUCTION

It would never have occurred to the author of this little volume to write the story of his life, for he realizes that he is but an ordinary person. He did so at the request of his Novice Master; the first duty of a novice in a Trappist monastery is to obey.

He has availed himself of this opportunity to thank the Lord God for his conversion, and to tell his brothers and sisters all that the Lord has done for him and how the Lord has had mercy on him.

He has addressed himself to humble men, seekers after truth. Every human intelligence desires to know, and every will seeks the good. The author has treated especially of that in his experience which, being universal, pertains to all; and what happened to him can if others likewise will it—happen to them.

To fall in love with God is the greatest of all romances; to seek Him, the greatest adventure; to find Him, the greatest human achievement.

The author acknowledges himself to be such only in a very secondary sense. What he relates, namely, the story of his conversion, is God's work; its accurate remembrance he sought and obtained (it seems to him) from God; finally, in narrating his recollections, he has leaned heavily upon the grace of God, mindful of his limited capabilities.

Moreover he knows that if souls of good will profit by this book, it will be because they have listened to its primary and true Author, the Lord God, speaking through a poor instrument. As Miss Rosalie Marie Levy has said in her autobiography: "He can and will make use of humble souls who desire not only to love Him themselves, but to bring others to know and love and serve Him too." God is a seeker of souls; He is present in the heart of each. He speaks to them from without through human instruments, but He also testifies—to those who are willing to hear Him—from within.

FOREWORD TO THE REVISED EDITION

There is widespread interest in stories of those whose search for the truth and for stable values leads to dramatic changes in their outlook and life-course. This is such a story, the story of a conversion. At the time when the radical change in my perspective and life occurred, I was a young man formed by a liberal, scientific, and agnostic tradition. I came from a Jewish background, the son of Jewish parents. I went from this background into the Roman Catholic Church. Then, as a psychiatrist, I entered and found enduring satisfaction in a society of contemplative monks, a community of the Cistercian Trappist Order. This is the Order of St. Benedict, St. Bernard, and Thomas Merton.

THE GLORY OF THY PEOPLE was in print for over twenty years. At the end of this period, after Vatican Council II, there was an upsurge of secularization amidst rapid social change. Religion was in rapid decline which some considered irreversible, particularly religion which emphasized the sacred. This decade announced "the death of God." Religious books were out-of-date, especially if they were not written in the current year. The confusion permeating secular society entered the Church.

The Vatican Council had just completed a wonderful work in fulfillment of the Church's mission to be the light of the world. It presented its understanding of the Church in terms which are appropriate for people of our time. It brought the Church into dialogue with the modern world and showed a sensitivity to the various issues which concern modern men and women. It addressed people who had no interest in religion, as well as non-Christians, non-Catholic Christians, and Catholics, with a view of finding common ground. It laid the foundation for cooperation and conversation among people of good-will. Its work continues to bear fruit.

xv

In 1968 I met a young Cistercian abbot who had just left the Order. Aware that I was a convert, he asked me: "But hasn't your faith been shaken?" No, it had not. Grace had prepared me for what was to take place. The confusion which has entered the Church, which reflects the confusion in society, is the same confusion out of which, little by little, I emerged in my search for truth. I had been immersed in the currents of the modern world, the same currents to which the Church opened itself in its renewal. The Holy Spirit led me, as it also led Vatican Council II, to understand their shortcomings and weaknesses, the soft bottom of the "modern mind."

These weaknesses are now being recognized in very diverse quarters, but especially by cultural critics. Some see signs of the emergence of a new age, the post-modern era characterized by religious revival and religious influence in national and world politics, in which religion will no longer be regarded as a strictly private affair.

The modern mind has recognized the dignity of each human life. It has recognized the right and need for members of society to participate in government and in their share of the fruits of the earth and of production. But it violates what it values. It creates a conscious cleavage between God and the human mind and heart, between God and his creation. Its science of the human mind and heart, and of society, is "valueless" and fosters what tends to become a valueless, purposeless life for the individual and society. Its benevolent mask has been rent by the tragedies of our age: the World Wars, the Holocaust and Hiroshima, totalitarian societies (including communistic societies), terrorism, crime, the legalized killing of the most innocent of human lives, the unborn. The barrier which the modern mind creates between God and the human heart leads to a barrier between people. The outrages to the 20th century conscience are an outcome of the modern mind. It is to the healing of these cleavages, to this disorder of the modern mind, that Vatican II addressed itself.

But what had happened to religion? Religion alone brings into focus the spiritual dimension and gives a firm rooting to moral values. And only moral values inspired by religion can make the political and the economic systems work to the advantage of all. According to cultural critics, modern theology (particularly, though not exclusively, Protestant liberal theology) set up separate spheres of influence between religion on the one hand and politics and science on the other. Religion became privatized, it was simply an affair of the heart. And even in the heart it was diminished. Liberal theology emptied biblical faith of its content. It accommodated biblical faith to the world and to the "modern mind," and separated an impoverished faith from life.

Liberal theology did not recognize the correct relation between faith and reason, despite its valuable attempts to develop a rationalized theology suited for our age, say these critics. This is precisely what, by the Father's grace, I found: the relation of faith and reason, not lessening, but mutually supporting, each other. I found a remedy: authentic religion joined with sound reason healing the separation of God and the human heart, of people from each other.

But has not religion itself, and in particular Christianity, been the cause of "religious wars," tyranny, oppression, persecution, racism? Yes, *inauthentic* religion and *inauthentic* Christianity certainly have.

True religion has been defined by the Hebrew prophet Amos as "walking humbly before the Lord thy God," and by James as "coming to the help of orphans and widows when they need it and keeping oneself uncontaminated by the world." If we are moving into a new mentality and world order which turns to a personal God, the Father, known through authentic tradition, then we are moving into authentic religion. Then we are entering into authentic Christianity, where genuine love and concern for the welfare of each, including their spiritual welfare, is truly paramount. Into this promised land, Vatican II leads the way.

In the course of my conversion, I realized that science, which limits itself to what can be sensed, not only as a basis from which its reasoning starts, but also as a limit beyond which its reasoning cannot go, abdicates the full use of reason. Yet only the harmony of faith, reason, and science provides a solid basis for a happy, fruitful life in correspondence with God's grace and in accordance with His plan, which seeks the harmony of His entire creation.

The particulars of the path of my conversion will not mark out a path for others. The way in which the Holy Spirit conducted me must perforce be presented here in a sketchy manner, without the full development which might render it more convincing. Nevertheless I trust it will be thought-provoking. It has proven interesting and helpful to others. The Holy Spirit led me out of contemporary errors to an outlook in which faith, reason (sound philosophy), science and modern advances are integrated. He guided me into a deep interior life. The need for such an integration and authentic interior life is being felt. This is shown by the polls.

George Gallup stated in April 1984 that the majority of Americans find themselves more interested in religion now than they were five years ago. They are looking more to religion than science (though I think both are needed) to solve the problems of the world. And on college campuses, there is a religious ferment. It is no longer considered sophisticated to be secular.

* * * * *

In revising this book, I have not found it necessary to make changes in the story of my conversion. After all, I was much closer to it then than I am now! And I still believe what I believed at the time of writing this book, that the Holy Spirit was bringing back to my mind what had taken place.

I have placed substantial additions in italics. Some of these mention recent scientific findings supporting the insights which occurred to me during my conversion. And I have provided an "Afterword" on the State of Israel. Its establishment I see as a sign of our times connected with the mystery of Israel. There are also appendices quoting passages of special interest from the documents of Vatican II.

In its document on non-Christian religions, Vatican Council II articulated the attitude of the Church to the Jewish religion, while inaugurating with it a dialogue. It rejected anti-Semitism: "The Church repudiates all persecutions against any man.....she deplores the hatred, persecutions, and displays of anti-Semitism directed against the Jews at any time and from any source."

In its document on religious liberty, Vatican II denounced any form of coercion with respect to religious belief. True faith comes from God and He honors human liberty, of which He is the author. Authentic conversion can come from Him alone. I have always believed this. In fact this book is a testimony to that belief. And in that spirit I would like to offer a caution. This book is not meant for believing Jews. To them it is apt to be offensive. Perhaps it can best help the Jewish-Christian dialogue by making Christians more sensitive to the Jewish roots of Christianity. Of course, Christians are to some extent aware of these roots.

Nevertheless, it must be admitted that there is a great deal of ignorance about the "mystery of Israel" despite Paul's warning: "Brothers, I do not want you to be ignorant of this mystery lest you be conceited: blindness has come upon part of Israel until the full number of Gentiles enter in, and then all Israel will be saved... God's gifts and his call are irrevocable" (Romans 11:25-29). As the time approaches for the collective return of the "branches" to their "own natural olive tree", of which Paul speaks in the preceding verse, it is important that Christians enter more deeply into an understanding of the mystery of Israel. In doing so, they will come to know better Christ, His Church, and our times—and perhaps also the future. Perhaps Scripture and prophecy is illustrated by the story of an individual whose life reflects that mystery.

To those who are seeking light on the path to God—and their number at the present time is legion—this book may indicate the way that one seeker took, and may share with them his findings. I do not pretend that it will show the way to the "post-modern age" or to the age of the new Israel, although human efforts in cooperation with divine wisdom will be necessary for their realization. I simply wish to offer a testimony to a friendship and to a Friend, and to share this friendship as much as possible.

THE ANALYTICAL SUMMARY

The summaries at the beginning of each chapter provide a key to the development of the story and of its truths. In addition, these sections are united and presented at the end of the text as a summary.

CHAPTER ONE

GOD IS NO LONGER
IN THE MIDST
OF HIS PEOPLE

(1) Resolved: never to abandon the Jewish religion; by becoming a Catholic this resolution is kept.

(2) The orthodox Jewish religion.

(3) Public High School: anti-Church, anti-religion; one teacher speaks in favor of God.

(1)

I was born in New York, August 6, 1909, of Jewish parents, and my early religious education was in the Reformed Jewish Synagogue. It was such as to imbue me with a great admiration for my persecuted people who, refusing to change their religion, were put to death crying, "Hear! O Israel! The Lord our God, the Lord is one!" I too would never be converted; I would never betray my religion no matter how I was persecuted. In becoming a Catholic I fulfilled this resolution as this story will show.

In these childhood days I gained from the Bible an impression of the nobility of the Jewish race and of a people, humble and spiritual, who talked with God, had Him in their midst and made sacrifices to Him in which they expressed their loving acknowledgment of His supreme dominion over them and all that was theirs. His converse with them was real. He spoke to the prophets, told the people what He expected of them, encouraged them by wonderful promises and miracles. He threatened them with punishment if they should turn from Him. Yet when they did, He took them back, again and again, with wonderful fatherly goodness, and He provided them with the means to repair the great injustices which, by these repeated infidelities, they had done to Him.

In comparison with the religion of the Bible, the religion of my experience seemed somehow deficient. The Rabbis under whom I studied did not talk as the representatives of this living God, nor did God any longer seem to be in the midst of His people. The promised Messiah was alluded to, but the Rabbis of the present did not have the same great expectation of His coming as had the teachers whose words I had read in the Bible. These impressions were not clearly defined in my mind, yet vaguely I felt that something had happened.

3

There was a sudden gap in the relations between God and His Chosen People—and the promise of the Messiah had apparently not yet been fulfilled.

In my early religious education I had been taught that God is one: I had learned His Ten Commandments and something of the history of God and the human race. The race had begun with Adam and Eve. Following their treasonable disobedience, they had been expelled by God from the Garden of Eden. The Jewish race had begun when God called Abraham. God had made Abraham's descendants to be His own people and He exercised a special care over them. When they were enslaved by Pharaoh in Egypt, God sent Moses to deliver them and gave him the power of working miracles.

I also learned something of the history of the Jewish people since the founding of the Christian religion. I formed the vague notion that their place in society as an object of ridicule and as a persecuted people was a consequence of the death of Jesus Christ. In the Middle Ages the Jews in Europe were set apart in ghettos, but with the enlightenment of modern times they had taken their rightful place in society. My religious education culminated in the ceremony of confirmation (Bar Mitzvah) when I was thirteen.

I had not formed a clear conception of the doctrine of the Jewish religion. Indeed, the teaching of different Rabbis was not in agreement. I had not received such an explanation of religious principles as would prepare me to withstand the attacks against religious truth which I was about to encounter.

(2)

Concerning the Orthodox Jewish religion, I received the impression that it consisted of many observances which were suitable for the time and conditions of civilization under which they had been given by God; these observances were not practicable in a modern world. Likewise, I had been taught by the Reformed Rabbis that one need not take the doctrine of the Jewish religion as strictly as did the Orthodox Jews. Thus, it was open to question whether the Bible was inspired by God or was merely of human tradition, Adam and Eve need not be accepted as the progenitors of the human race, the miracles of Moses might be explained as natural phenomena, etc.

(3)

As a result of public high school education, religion became even less of a conscious force in my life. There was no religious instruction; and religion, especially the Catholic religion, was sometimes slighted. For example, in my history course, I was taught that Europe had been the slave of a Church which fettered the minds of the people by the authority of the Bible, but that a great reformation had occurred, in which this darkness and slavery of mind were overthrown, and in which art, science and reason were liberated. In science, I was taught the theory of evolution. Religious fanatics, the Fundamentalists, had opposed the progress of science, but this was of passing moment. I was impressed with the notion of an impersonal God, Who was identified somehow with natural law; a Being without intelligence, interest in man, or power to converse with, or help him. This idea seemed to agree with my experience of men and women and their conduct. God was not manifest to me in the world, in the conduct of men or women, or in their conversation. He was referred to occasionally by the phrase, "God bless you," from a sincerely well-wishing relative. I did indeed have a grandfather whose life showed that he took God very seriously. He was a pious, orthodox Jew, and I respected him greatly. However, as he lived in California and I in New York, he did not enter deeply into my life.

One teacher, only, in high school, spoke out in God's favor—and her one statement, coming at the end of my high school training, outweighed much that was negative. She said that the majority of scientists did believe in God; they did not find an inconsistency between the truths of science and of religion. Nevertheless, the sense of a living God dwelling with and conversing with His people now seemed to me merely a childish impression.

CHAPTER TWO

SEARCH FOR THE KINGDOM
OF TRUTH

(1) At the University of Michigan: discovery of the want of unity in modern education.

(2) At the University of Berlin: glimpses of the secret Kingdom of Truth.

(3) Friends on the way to the goal.

(4) At Medical School; Aristotelian Philosophy, St. Thomas Aquinas and the changeless Truth: what is wanting in modern education is the knowledge of true philosophy.

(5) At the University of Chicago: Dr. Robert Maynard Hutchins takes the lead in modern education by introducing into it the knowledge of true philosophy.

(6) Logic and Metaphysics: the existence of truth, the knowledge of natural principles.

(7) Doubts concerning evolution: failure of the attempt to explain creation without admitting a Creator.

(8) Origin of the human race: not from apes but from first human parents.

(9) Immaterial ideas require an immaterial power of reason, an immaterial and hence incorruptible soul.

(10) The Angels: complete immaterial intelligent beings.

(11) The Five Proofs of the Existence of God.

(12) Aristotle's wisdom, knowledge, science and logic; his devotion to truth. St. Thomas' perfect understanding of and agreement with the philosophy of Aristotle; his similar devotion to truth; his application of the philosophic method to the examination of the revealed truths of the Catholic religion. I can no longer despise the Catholic Faith nor refuse to examine it.

(13) The Infallible Teaching Authority of the Catholic Church; the logical invulnerability of its Faith: all its doctrine must be divinely true if any of it is divinely true; for it is proposed on God's authority, on God's Word.

(14) Moral values are real: the Ten Commandments express the natural moral law.

(15) Human Happiness cannot be found in creatures, but only in God; virtue is the power of attaining Happiness; grace is the gift of this power.

(16) Discovery of the insufficiency of philosophy and natural means for achieving Happiness: the Gap.

(17) God bridges the Gap for me. "Oh, you of little faith."

(1)

After finishing high school, I entered the University of Michigan. During my studies there I had no contact with religion or religious ideas. The great ideal appeared to be the accumulation of knowledge; and knowledge (but not religious truth) seemed to me the real basis for individual and social perfection; to know truth and to put it into action, to regulate all human affairs through it. There even seemed to be a science—eugenics—for the regulation of the propagation of the human race and its constant improvement. I sensed an immense capacity for improvement in myself as well as in the human race, and it seemed to me that nothing should be permitted to hinder it, that no ideal less than a constant striving after perfection should be accepted.

In the University of Michigan I acquired much information. Although I appreciated the wonderful facilities of this great university and enjoyed the kind, neighborly midwestern spirit, I felt that something was wanting: something that would provide unity and order, something which would discipline the power of intelligence.

One day I appealed to my German professor, an elderly man who treated his students in a spirit of fellowship and who seemed possessed of wisdom. After listening gravely to my account of my state of mind he laughed and said, "All right, I'll tell you what to do. Read Theodore Drieser's *American Tragedy.*" I did—and despaired of help from my professor.

The idea of spending my third collegiate year at a foreign university occurred to me. I considered that in the Old World I might find what I sensed to be lacking in my education, and decided to study at the University of Berlin.

9

(2)

One year later, in the spring of 1928, I was in an omnibus speeding up Kurfurstendamm. I was finishing my studies at Berlin. I had not been altogether successful in learning the German language, but had acquired enough to follow the lectures and courses. As the bus passed one of the street cafes, I saw three young Germans from the University. They were talking earnestly. I liked them: they were sincere and intelligent. They had a way of argument which was free from contention; an affable way of asking questions, and challenging each other's premises and reasonings. They were, it seemed to me, in love with truth. As the omnibus passed by, I was touched deeply by the picture of their friendly intimacy. Some day perhaps, I felt expectantly, I too would have such friends.

Something of such a friend I had in Doctor Lichner, a psychiatrist. He wanted to learn to perfect his English and had applied to the University for a tutor. His wife, a dentist, invited me to take dinner with them on my visits. In return, I spent most of the fees in presents of candy or flowers.

Doctor Lichner was interested in philosophy, art, architecture, and in a wide variety of subjects. "Psychiatry," I thought, "must include some knowledge of whatever touches the human mind or heart."

During this year I was especially attracted by the course on the History of Philosophy. Philosophy presented ideas about life, the soul, truth and justice—and through these ideas I caught glimpses of a secret kingdom.

(3)

That Christmas (1928) I was on another bus. This was a Greyhound chartered by medical and dental students of the University of Michigan on their way to New York for the vacation. The students were congenial. Two, both Jewish, impressed me particularly: Herbert Schwartz and Herbert Ratner.

On the return trip to Ann Arbor, the same group of boys were in the bus. I had with me the notes which I had taken in my philosophy course in Berlin and was passing the time by ruminating over them. The impression of an Inner Kingdom, in which truth and justice were realities, returned. That night I found myself in earnest conversation with Herbert Ratner, and as the bus rolled on through the darkness, I was telling him in a low voice of these convictions while he nodded seriously, understandingly. Also during this trip, Herbert Ratner and Herbert Schwartz became friends, and at the University thereafter we three were frequently together. I admired Herbert Schwartz's wonderful power of mind; and I was very much impressed with his solicitude in tutoring one of the poorer students who lived in his rooming house. He had an almost maternal care, as if to say, "Now, don't worry about this; you'll get through all right." And I, seeing him so content with the company of one of the dullest and most ordinary students, began to realize with confusion my tendency to desire association with those who were exceptional.

Herbert Ratner likewise had an admirable love for people. When, one Christmas Eve, little Frances (the landlady's twelve-year-old daughter) was left alone, he was touched by her sadness and spent the whole evening reading Irish stories to her. To both of these young men, one of them engaged in research work in the medical school, the other a pre-medical student, life and people were to be taken earnestly. Neither did they spare themselves. They seemed determined to overcome their defects. Their goal perhaps was not yet in sight, but they were on their way to it.

(4)

The following year, in September 1929, I entered medical school at the University of Michigan. In the next few years when I met Herbert Schwartz in New York City I saw that he was advancing to that unseen goal. During this time, while I continued medical studies, Herbert had dropped out of medical school and was studying for his Ph.D. at Columbia. He had found the philosophical tradition. His power of reasoning had become more disciplined. Following the philosophical tradition backwards (I surmise) he had discovered the great philosophers, the Catholic Doctors and Fathers. More than this, he had discovered God. He had a sweetness and peace which was more marked now than ever before.

A digression and review will make clear, I think, the reason for my responsiveness to these discussions with Herbert. As everyone, at certain moments, has an intuition that there must be some great purpose to life, so I too had often felt this. But that God was this purpose never occurred to me in my conscious reasoning. In my boyhood, as I have remarked, the Bible had left me with the impression of a living God Who dwelt with His people, talked with them, told them what He expected of them and promised and gave them great rewards. However, as I advanced in my religious training, these impressions had not been strengthened and confirmed by the teaching of the Rabbis—rather the contrary. To them, and after a while to me, this was the God of the past. Certainly there was no longer a Moses to whom God gave explicit instructions on how to lead His people, nor a Samuel to whom God spoke and who answered, "Speak, Lord, for thy servant heareth." I did not reflect further, but accepted the views of the Rabbis.

In high school and college, God had slipped further from view, and a new ideal had formulated itself in my mind: it seemed that through the progressive accumulation of knowledge, the human race would be able to perfect itself and to order and arrange its own affairs. After two years at college, however, I had the personal experience that as my knowledge accumulated, less and less order prevailed in it. Subsequently a glimmer of light had appeared to me: apparently besides the knowledge of sensible facts, a higher knowledge, the knowledge of their principles, or philosophy, existed, by means of which these sensible facts could be judged, and to which ideas concerning them and concerning the meaning of life could be referred. At the University of Berlin I had been attracted to the study of philosophy. During my conversations with Dr. Lichner, psychiatry had appealed to me as a practical profession, in the course of which I would be able to pursue this study in connection with an understanding of the persons whose disorders I would be called upon to treat.

On returning to the United States, I took up the study of medicine as a preparation for psychiatry. In my experience with Herbert Schwartz I had seen more clearly that the way to truth led, not through an accumulation of knowledge, but through reasoning from facts to principles.

Now in the discussions with Herbert in New York City (which took place during my third year in medical school) I sensed that he had arrived at basic truth through his studies of philosophy and theology. To him God was not a blind natural force, nor a God of the past, but a living and intelligent Being. "God," he had said, "is intelligence." This I found a very satisfactory statement. He had not spoken to me about theology nor—beyond that remark—about God. Instead we had a long argument over the nature of the mind. Against my contention that the mind, consciousness, could be fully explained as the activity of the brain, Herbert argued that in addition the facts concerning mental activity and consciousness required a spiritual, intellectual substance, the soul, with a power of understanding and reasoning. At the time I was not convinced by his argument; yet I felt that through his knowledge of philosophy he had attained a more perfect and comprehensive view than that presented by the scientists and authors I had studied.

One night we had a long discussion on philosophy. Herbert, in three or four hours, outlined the Aristotelian philosophy. I was very much impressed; in those three hours I understood a great deal. Further conversations revealed that it was not in Aristotle but in St. Thomas Aquinas' writings that Herbert had found the most perfect presentation of truth. In him, Plato, Aristotle and St. Augustine had been harmonized. St. Thomas had concluded that Aristotle knew the truth in the realm of philosophy. Herbert had concluded that St. Thomas knew the truth in the realm of philosophy and theology. For my part, I had found that what was lacking in modern education was knowledge of true philosophy. I knew nothing of theology or of St. Thomas. But I did begin to realize that the modern idea of progress could be very deceptive when applied to advance in knowledge of eternal truth. For I saw that this was not inevitably brought about by the passage of time. The passage of time has brought with it wonderful advances in non-philosophic knowledge. It has brought with it wonderful technical apparatus, such as the microscope, by means of which what was formerly hidden—like bacteria—can be seen, studied and understood. Through my conversations with Herbert I began to realize more clearly what I had dimly perceived in Berlin: modern science has not added any notable knowledge to the sciences of logic, metaphysics, ethics and natural theology since their objects (reason, being, human acts, God) are not disclosed by material instruments, but were just as evident to the ancients as to us. In this realm a mind disciplined in reasoning abstractly (yet in strict conformity with the concrete facts) is the sole instrument necessary for the attainment of truth—and of changeless truth. I realized that our very love of originality and novelty, and our sense of having advanced beyond the knowledge of our predecessors, tend to lead us to reject ancient truths for new errors.

My attraction to philosophy had now been inflamed to an ardor, and when Herbert spoke of his teacher's interest in collaborating with a medical expert who would apply philosophical reasoning to the analysis of medicine, I was enthusiastic. I had hoped to reach the study of philosophy through psychiatry; now I had a short cut. I expected to finish my medical studies the next year and then collaborate with Professor Richard McKeon. That spring, in the fourth year of my medical studies, Herbert was in Ann Arbor, and with two other friends (of one, Bill Gorman, I will speak later) we formed a little class. My philosophical studies were proceeding in earnest. In addition to this, Herbert and I had several discussions on the theory of medicine. On the basis of these discussions and a review of the opinions of modern medical experts on the fundamental concepts of medicine and disease, I had written an outline of the direction I would pursue in making a philosophical study of medicine. This had been submitted through the kindness of Professor McKeon whom I had met in New York, to the Josiah Macy, Junior, Foundation with the hope of obtaining a grant of money to pursue this project in collaboration with him. These arrangements, however, had not been completed and as I had not made an effort to obtain an internship, I now began to worry. Herbert saw this and in a kindly way said, "Have faith."

I had no clear idea of Providence but intuitively I saw what he meant: we are not sufficient to arrange our future; we are dependent on God's Providence. Therefore, depend on His help. For the first time I *did* have confidence in God. My anxiety abated. Soon the arrangements for the following year were completed.

(5)

The next two years, 1934 to 1936, I spent at the University of Chicago. Professor McKeon had been appointed Dean of the Division of Humanities. My work with him had been subsidized by the Josiah Macy, Junior Foundation, and he was tutoring me in philosophy. Herbert Schwartz and Bill Gorman, another friend, had also received appointments at the University.

President Hutchins was encouraging the development of a more unified and intelligent educational system. The scientific division had developed a co-ordinated syllabus. In the Division of Humanities, philosophy was receiving a more important place. Dean McKeon taught Aristotle's *Ethics* and *Logic*, Plato's *Republic*, and the intellectual history of the middle ages. Dr. Hutchins and Dr. Adler conducted an "Honors" course in the Classics, in which were read Plato, Aristotle, St. Thomas Aquinas, Galileo, Newton, the Old and New Testaments, and other great works of science, philosophy and theology. The modern preconceptions of the

students were subjected to the scrutiny of reason; the
students were obliged to form, express and defend their
opinions. Dr. Adler and Dr. Malcolm Sharpe conducted a
"pre-law" class in which the students were trained in
grammar, rhetoric and logic, and in which philosophy,
morality and theology were discussed.

I found this educational program very stimulating. The
need of modern education, as envisioned by these men, for
order, agreed with the need I had experienced at the
University of Michigan. And here, the power inherent in
traditional philosophy for providing order for modern sciences was recognized.

In Dr. Adler, Dr. Hutchins and Dean McKeon, I found men
who, like Herbert Schwartz, had, in virtue of native talent
and traditional philosophical training, the ability to rise from
facts to principles and thence to obtain a rational bird's-eye
view of great tracts of subject matter.

*Dr. Hutchins had an unusual vision. He was Dean of the
Yale Law School at the age of 28. After he became President of
the University of Chicago, he brought there Mortimer Adler
and Richard McKeon to help him in the implementation of
his ideas.*

*It was Dr. Hutchins' hope to make theology and traditional
philosophy central in the university. Traditional philosophy would provide a common language. One day Bill
Gorman, who incidentally was the tutor of Dr. Hutchins'
young daughter, said that Dr. Hutchins had a list of thirteen
of us who were educated in Aristotelian philosophy as well
as in modern disciplines: medicine, mathematics, music,
literature, languages, history, etc.*

*It became obvious that this project would not be capable of
realization. Instead Dr. Hutchins' ideas were channeled into
the development of the Great Books program for adult
education, and into support of an experimental college, St.
John's in Annapolis, Maryland, carried on by two friends of
his, McKeon's and Adler's: Stringfellow Barr and Scott
Buchanan.*

The basis of the curriculum of St. John's College was the Great Books program. Other colleges and universities were to be influenced by this idea.

To many, these ideas and the "intellectual love of God" about which Hutchins wrote at this time, seem regressive even though they did not arise out of a lack of esteem for contemporary disciplines, but from a realization that these needed to be balanced by the cultivation of traditional philosophy and theology. Isn't there a tendency amongst us to look upon our predecessors as if they were—almost—a lower species? Or, if they do seem to have said something worthwhile, as if they were precocious children? We admit that though they lacked the maturity and developed consciousness of us moderns, they did occasionally have a bright idea.

It is incontestable that there has been a tremendous scientific and technological advance, and especially in the twentieth century. I do believe that there has been positive cultural developments in many other areas too. But I came to think that by mastering the thought of our predecessors we could have a more far-reaching vision.

Parenthetically let me quote Msgr. John Tracy Ellis, who might be called the dean of American Catholic intellectuals, writing in America, *October 6, 1984: "Catholic institutions, it seems to me, should not be expected to attempt to compete with any degree of success in fields such as medicine, engineering and technology. If they fail to make an impressive showing in these areas it hardly touches the 'heart of the matter' of the Christian educational tradition. That lies rather in the liberal arts and the humanities. As the late Robert Maynard Hutchins, then president of the University of Chicago, once reminded a Catholic audience, it is there that Catholics should recognize a domain that is peculiarly their own. He declared, 'The best service Catholic education can perform for the nation and all education is to show that the intellectual tradition can again be made the heart of higher education.'"*

*In particular I came to believe that we must go back
beyond the modern period and the thought patterns which it
has engendered and bequeathed to us (without our hardly
realizing it) to reach a stratum of thought that has philosophic truth in philosophic critical realism as its objective.
This stratum of thought I had found in Aristotle and St.
Thomas. I was not interested in their ideas as the ideas of
Aristotle, or the ideas of Thomas—that would have been
merely an interest in the history of ideas. I was interested in
their thought insofar as it led to an apprehension of the truth
ascertainable by reason—which is the object of philosophy.*

*I came through this discipline to a criticism of presupposi-
tions embedded in the modern mentality, presuppositions
which I had shared. One of these has to do with considering
the scientific method to be the only, or the most privileged,
avenue to truth. In the course of my medical education, I
spent a year doing basic medical research in order to
acquaint myself more thoroughly with the scientific method
(and was awarded an M.A. in Materia Medica and Thera-
peutics for doing so.) I have never wavered in my devotion to
science and its method for the investigation of scientific
questions. Rather what had happened in the progress I am
describing was the discovery, beginning in Berlin, that
certain questions do not pertain to science, but to another
field, namely philosophy, and others to theology, and that we
must use the method appropriate to each field in the pursuit
of truth.*

(6)

As my studies in philosophy proceeded, I saw clearly that
truth, eternal changeless truth, existed. I saw that it was
attainable, contrary to the opinion of skeptics who assert
that no truth is certain. I realized that its foundation is in the
really existing order of being, contrary to the idealists and
subjectivists who, as I had found, place an impassable gulf
between our minds and things existing outside our minds. I
now discovered that there is in each natural thing a natural
principle, the thing's nature—e.g., human nature in men as

their principle. The definition of the thing states it, the name signifies it. This nature does not exist apart from individuals, it is not a thing in an individual, but it is what individuals of the same kind have in common. From it proceed all the properties and powers of the thing—in men and women, e.g., their human reason and will, the bodily powers which sustain life, etc. The intellect perceives this natural principle as well as all the properties of things (known first through sense); and it also perceives the order between these properties—thus, I understood, scientific knowledge is formulated. When this knowledge agrees with the reality to which it refers, the mind, which possesses it, possesses truth.

(7)

During this period of time I was forced to re-examine many of the ideas which I had taken for granted in my earlier education, e.g., concerning the origin of the universe and the human race, the nature of the mind, the existence of immaterial beings. I had once firmly believed that the world began, *by itself*, from clouds of matter which gradually formed themselves into the present universe. I also believed that simple living organisms had arisen from non-living matter under especially favorable conditions, that from these the more complex species had developed through the course of ages, and finally that from lower species, humans had arisen, through certain intermediate stages. These intermediate stages, according to the theory I accepted, had left certain clues of their existence before they became extinct. The wonderful gradation of living things and the apparent "recapitulation" of the course of evolution in the embryological development of the higher animals and man, had appealed to me as proof of evolution. When, in medical school, an anatomist-surgeon who had done special work in embryology had laughed at this theory, I was taken aback. However, he based his rejection of it upon embryological specimens, and pointed out that Haeckel, who had proposed these views with great violence in the nineteenth century, had even gone so far as to introduce falsified evidence.

During my studies in philosophy, however, I reconsidered the validity of the theory of evolution. Embryological recapitulation did not prove but supposed the evolutionary theory. The supposition of evolution has no *direct* evidence and no *direct* logical proof to sustain it. In the recorded history of the world no instance of a species has been known to give rise to an offspring of a higher species. On the contrary, when living offspring which differ from the parent stock are produced by breeding experiments—for example, hybrids—they tend to lose their fertility (the mule) or to revert in their characteristics to the parent stock. Analogies between the successive stages of embryonic development and the gradation of living beings exist in the nature of things, without requiring evolution as an explanation. For both must proceed from simple to complex forms, from unicellular to multicellular. Both require in the higher members of their series organs and systems. The theory of rudimentary organs did not have sufficient evidence to support it (for example, the supposed rudiments of gills in air-breathing mammalian embryos never show any tendency to become respiratory organs, but are probably associated with the development of non-respiratory organs). So with other evidences of evolution. The vermiform appendix, like the thymus in man, proves, not that man has remnants of organs signifying his origin from lower ancestral species, but that structures not used by the fully formed individual, perhaps useful in its embryological development, atrophy. The discovery of supposedly intermediate forms, including hominids, in the "evolution of the human species" does not prove that the human species arose from these forms.

As I studied the first principles of natural things, my understanding of their simplicity and uniformity increased and, with clearer ideas, I realized the intrinsic impossibility of a natural evolution of species. Species which are really distinct have an essential difference—color, for example, is only an accidental difference constituting different races of men, who are united nonetheless in all their essential characters and characteristics in one human species. Again, a natural change proceeds in accordance with a natural principle, and is determinate—i.e., proceeds in the same way. Each being has as its natural principle the nature or species by which it is constituted as a certain kind of thing, and which is the principle of all its natural operations. Reproduction is a natural operation, proceeding from and in accordance with the nature of a living being, and it also must therefore be determinate—the offspring must be of the same nature as the parents. Thus evolution of new species as a natural process is impossible. Neither could it occur by chance, since the more perfect (a man, for example) could not arise by chance from the less perfect (a lower animal). Again, an effect cannot exceed the perfection and power of its cause, as all experience and science prove. But the perfect design of a new species can only be accounted for by supposing the Creator as a cause, Who has the perfect Intelligence to design each kind of natural being, and the all-powerful Will to execute His design—by creation—an act befitting Divine Nature. I understood that the addition in the theory of evolution of an extended period of time—an age—during the course of which what otherwise is inconceivable could be supposed to occur, does not remove the difficulty. For if the evolution of a new species is to occur at all, then at some one generation a new nature would arise in some individual, without an adequate cause, and would be the offspring of parents of a different and lower species.

The question of evolution, to the extent that it can be investigated scientifically, is a scientific question. It has philosophic aspects, insofar as it involves philosophic suppositions and the causality of God, which reason can investigate but science cannot. Finally it has theological aspects which exceed the limits of reason, insofar as there has been a divine Revelation concerning the origin of the human race and the universe.

The conclusions which I reached and which I am remembering in this narrative were reached without reference to Revelation. At this time I did not believe in Revelation. These conclusions are not part of the teaching of the Catholic

Church. Catholics and Catholic theologians have the same openness to the scientific evidence for evolution as non-Catholics. Pius XII taught that Catholics were free to investigate the evolution of the human body from lower species. Catholic doctrine does hold that each human soul is the direct creation of God.

In April 1985 a meeting of fifteen scientists, philosophers, and theologians was held in Rome under the auspices of the Congregation of the Office of Doctrine of the Faith on the subject of evolution. Written reports of participants are forthcoming. Meanwhile one of the chairmen and organizers of this meeting, Professor Low, a scientist and philosopher, has said that evolution as a goal-directed process is acceptable philosophically, while evolution as a series of random events is not.

An example of evolution as a goal-directed process has been given theological expression by Karl Rahner. According to his explanation, if "hominisation through evolution" occurs, then it does so because God supports intimately, from within, the creature as a mutable being in its movement of self-development and self-transcendence. In the case of man this divine causality, operating together with the creature's movement of becoming something beyond itself, is the same thing as immediate creation; i.e what is new has God as its source (Evolution. Hominisation. In Sacramentum Mundi). *This example of Rahner's explanation of evolution applies to all natural beings, but Rahner points out that this "evolutionary" view can only analogously be applied to human history, human societies, and the history of mind or spirit, for the essential differences between these kinds of beings and non-human beings have to be taken into account.*

But what is the scientific evidence that evolution has occurred? When Charles Darwin published his ORIGIN OF SPECIES in 1859, he was aware that the evidence in the geological record for his theory of evolution was lacking. He predicted that research would fill in the gaps between species.

According to a new school of evolutionists, lives devoted by generations of scientists to this endeavor have not filled in the gaps "not in the case of man, of the horse, of any species." Hence they have called an end to this fruitless search. What the geological record does show, they affirm, is that species begin suddenly and remain constant throughout their history until they become extinct. (Of course this biological stability, the most universal finding of biology, does not deny the evident fact that a species undergoes variations in adaptation to its environment, for example to climactic conditions).

To accord with the facts, Stephen Jay Gould, Harvard geologist, author of EVER SINCE DARWIN, and Niles Eldredge, paleontologist at the American Museum of Natural History, proposed the Theory of Punctuated Equilibrium in scientific articles in 1972 and 1977 (see NEW EVOLUTION-ARY TIMETABLE by Steven M. Stanley, Basic Books, mentioned in an article in Newsweek, March 29, 1982, pp. 44–49, captioned "Enigmas of Evolution.") This theory of evolution is called PUNCTUATED because of the sudden beginnings of species, and EQUILIBRIUM because once a species appears in the geological record, it remains constant (until it becomes extinct).

This left open the question: how then did the human race originate? It was a question which science had not answered, and I felt the creation of two parents of the race best explained its origin.

(8)

Likewise, I now realized that the theory of development of the universe from nebulae was inadequate. If out of clouds of matter the heavens and earth had gradually taken form, plants, animals and men gradually come to be, this itself would be a wonderful thing and could not be accounted for without supposing a God Who had endowed matter with such wonderful properties. It was evident to me that just as plants, animals and men had a separate origin, directly from

God, so the inanimate universe itself had been created, for it could not have brought itself into being.

The Big Bang Theory holds that the universe began at a precise moment in an explosion, a fireball, some twelve to twenty billion years ago. All the stuff of the universe was present in this exploding dense mass of intense light and trillions of degrees of heat. Some force, unknown and unknowable to science, brought this fireball into existence— and that was the beginning of time.

In 1948 Alpher and Herman stated that if the universe began in a fireball as the Big Bang Theory held, a radiation proceding from the glow of this fireball should be detectable coming uniformly from all parts of the universe.

In 1965 Penzias and Wilson detected with a large horn antenna radiation coming uniformly from all quarters of the universe. This confirmed the prediction made in 1948 by Alpher and Herman. This has been accepted as a confirmation of the Big Bang Theory. (See God and the Astronomers, *by the astronomer Robert Jastrow, W.W.Norton & Co., New York, 1978, paperback, 136 pages.)*

If science cannot prove the existence of God, although reason can, it is because science has so defined itself as to exclude from its purview what is not material. Reason can also see the suitability of the natural order to human needs; and hence the manifestation of God's wisdom and kindness, and the natural foundation of His care for human beings.

(9)

I was now able to appreciate the inadequacy of the materialistic account of human nature. At the University of Berlin I had attended Dr. Koehler's classes. His experiments with apes had led him to recognize their ability to grasp a situation. But they had no power to rise from situations that they sensed, to general principles. Obviously there is some additional power in man, a power to form ideas, which is exactly what makes him a human being as opposed to an animal. Science, which concerns itself with things which can be weighed and measured, has not been able to discover this power to form ideas because ideas cannot be weighed and measured. Ideas are immaterial; they have no quantity, shape, color. Yet they exist and are evidence of a real power of understanding, which like themselves must be immaterial. For the acts of a power have the same nature as the power. A material act, such as walking, proceeds from a material power, in this case the power of locomotion; an immaterial act, such as an idea, proceeds from an immaterial power, the intellect. So must the power of choice with regard to acting or not acting in accordance with one's ideas be immaterial. So, finally, must the very substance in which the powers are rooted be immaterial. Thus the facts prove the existence of the soul. It follows also that if the soul is immaterial it is not able to change and die; consequently it must be immortal. I had discovered the reality of the soul and its immortality, and, since the body dies and the soul does not, the possibility *of a spiritual existence free from bodily conditions. "Near-death experiences" confirm this conclusion. Compare* Life After Life, *Raymond A. Moody, Jr., M.D., Bantam Books, Inc. N.Y., N.Y.,1976. Paperback, 184 pages.* My principal difficulties in regard to the human mind and the explanation of its operations were now solved. Just as the soul informs the body, with which it constitutes one unity, one species, so its powers of reason and will (capable of a completely spiritual operation—such as must occur after death and the loss of the body) are during life associated in their action with the sensitive powers of the mind (external and internal senses, imagination and memory) which have bodily organs (brain, external senses) as their instruments.

Thus we do not form or use ideas, in intellectual thought or reasoning, without the association of images or phantasms derived from our sensitive experience (i.e., from seeing, hearing, etc.), from which these ideas were first abstracted by the natural operation of the active intellect.

The neurosurgeon, Dr. Wilder Penfield, spent a life-time mapping out the functions of the brain during brain operations. He was searching for the central regulating mechanism of the brain, which would explain the functions of the mind. He found the highest brain mechanism (in the thalamus), without which the mind could not operate, which is turned off during sleep and on during consciousness. But he also found that the brain, a computer, needed a programmer, the mind, of a different nature and not reducible to the brain, which could operate the computer through the highest brain mechanism. This programmer, the mind, could only be accounted for by a spiritual element, which has a continuous existence, whether we are asleep or awake. He recounts his search and conclusions in his book, The Mystery of the Mind, *Wilder Penfield, Princeton University Press, Princeton, N.J. 1975. 123 pages.*

(10)

The conception of spiritual beings was suggested by the gradation of beings:

material inanimate beings

animated material beings (plants and animals)

beings composite of matter and spirit (human beings)

spiritual beings (angels)

Their existence was affirmed by Aristotle, who attributed the movement of the heavenly bodies to their activity.

Previously I had shared the modern contempt concerning the existence of angels. Pictures of them in human form with great wings had been represented to me as ridiculous, and did strike me so. The existence, however, of spiritual beings who, unlike man, are not a union of body and soul but purely spiritual, exercising spiritual powers of intelligence and will, became for me a clear and intelligible concept. Thus when I met with Aristotle's theory of the movement of stars and planets, it did not seem as strange as it would previously have appeared to me. As in a human being the spiritual powers of intelligence and will are capable of moving and directing the material powers of the body, as for example in speech, so the movement of the heavenly bodies, Aristotle postulated, is initiated and directed by the angels, utilizing a spiritual energy far exceeding that found in the human spirit because of the condition of their nature. Aristotle had called these angels the "Intelligences." Modern scientists, on the other hand, find that the movement of the stars, planets, etc., can be accounted for within the order of physical nature itself.

My interest in Aristotle never led me to give the slightest credence to such of his scientific conclusions as were outdated by the advance of scientific investigation. Such was not the case of the 17th century "Aristotelians" who held to Aristotle's astronomical views despite emerging contrary evidence. In so doing they violated Aristotle's method, and hence were not truly Aristotelian.

I had found the answers to questions which had spontaneously arisen in my mind in the course of my education, but which until now had remained unanswered. Many natural scientists agree on the answers. Modern philosophy has largely abdicated this, its own domain, and given up the question and the answer. God has created the universe, for Himself, and adapted the natural order to man's needs, in His Wisdom and in His Providence for men. Matter itself was created by God, as were men in the persons of our first parents (as now seemed to me most reasonable to believe). Individuals of the various species and genera had a separate creation, at least those which are really specifically and generically distinct and of a different order of perfection— i.e., which have distinct natural principles (a distinct foundation of all their special properties)—as have the mammals, birds, the amphibians, fish, insects. Man has as his specific principle an immaterial and hence immortal soul, and its chief powers are the reason and will, immaterial as are their acts.

(11)

At the University of Chicago these questions were not abandoned; nor was the knowledge of God. On the contrary, here I found a view of God different from that commonly held in modern circles. Thus, Dr. Hutchins spoke of the intellectual love of God. Again, Dr. Adler discussed the five proofs of His existence given by St. Thomas Aquinas. These proofs were certain. Aristotle, on the basis of natural science and philosophy, had proven the existence of God. Through these proofs, I began to understand better the marvelous order in the development of the universe. This order presupposes a plan and this plan, a mind, and this mind, God. A Divine Mind which could bring material things into existence out of nothingness, and sustain their existence; which could give each kind of being a proper nature, such as minerals, plants, animals and men have; a Divine Mind which can move them by native motion, giving to plants their innate and natural development and reproduction; giving to animals their sensing and seeking of sensible objects, and giving men and women their understanding and choosing and seeking things known by the intelligence. Every *merely* possible being (every being which at some time did not exist, was a merely possible being at that time) must be brought into existence through a previously existing actual being, and the universe, with its series of material and immaterial beings, by the pre-existing and always actual God. Again, the reasonableness of the Biblical account of the creation of the universe and of Adam and Eve was evident, and also the unreasonableness of the theory that man began as a chance variation from the stock of lower animals.

Due to my acquaintance with the thought of St. Thomas I now also had a better conception of God, and of the way the mind attains its knowledge of God. Thus I discovered that there were two ways of having natural knowledge about the infinite, unknowable God. One is by way of analogical affirmation. Since all created things were made by Him, their beauty, goodness and truth must be a dim reflection of the infinite Beauty and Truth of their Author. The order, law and perpetuity of natural things give glimpses of the Divine order, law and perpetuity. The intelligence, freedom of will and purpose of human beings reflect the Divine Intelligence and Will which had made them in its own image. On the other hand, certain things could be said about God negatively. Since He is Infinite and all His attributes are Infinite, nothing limited could be true of Him. Thus, to identify Him with creation, as if created things were God and part of His Being, as the theory of Pantheism does, is unreasonable.

(12)

As time went on, I began to consider, besides the truths of the natural order, the truths of religion, and these in connection with the Catholic Church and its Faith. That I did so, arose from the great esteem I had conceived for St. Thomas Aquinas. Herbert Shwartz said that when he found himself in disagreement with Thomas he would set aside his own opinion to consider Thomas'. This is the opposite of the natural tendency to listen to pre-moderns only insofar as they agree with us.

In place of confusion concerning first truths, resulting from an education exclusive of true philosophy and religious teaching, I now had true conceptions of the universe, man, God, etc. I was gratefully devoted to philosophy, therefore, and realized that its fullest and clearest expression was in the works of St. Thomas.

My esteem for St. Thomas was strengthened by his unanimity with Aristotle. As my acquaintance with Aristotle progressed, my respect for him had grown. At first I had been critical of his work because his scientific knowledge, for example, in his biology, was imperfect, and in accordance with the contemporary prejudice regarding our predecessors, I suspected a deficiency in his spirit of observation and experimentation. After discussing Aristotle's biology with Herbert I had come to realize that his method was sound. Personal knowledge of his biology led me to realize what Linnaeus, Charles Darwin and others have enthusiastically affirmed. Aristotle was a great scientific investigator. In addition I realized what wonderful use he made of his investigations (hampered as they were by lack of the technical facilities available to the modern research worker) in drawing with penetrating insight conclusions appropriate to his findings. He had in fact constituted in outline the various sciences: physics, chemistry, biology, psychology, astronomy, ethics, metaphysics, logic, natural theology.

What would his wonderful mind not have been able to do if he had as a basis for his reasoning contemporary scientific information! He attained the truth in his formulation of those sciences whose data are obtainable in ordinary experience, such as logic and metaphysics. Of course even in respect to philosophic sciences, his work was subject to further improvements. Indeed Thomas Aquinas had perfected these disciplines, using the method of Aristotle, a method which is itself a refinement of common sense. I attributed his facility and relative inerrancy in philosophy to two qualities—first his thorough understanding of the principles and rules of reason—logic (which he comprehensively formulated) and his use of this knowledge to rectify and direct all his reasoning, and secondly, the cause of this uniformity: his love and devotion to the truth, which would not tolerate passion, prejudice or imperfection. These qualities I found present in St. Thomas. His commentaries on Aristotle's works revealed to me how completely he had understood his mind. The attitude which I had formed concerning Aristotle, I found manifested also by St. Thomas. He designates Aristotle: "*the* Philosopher." At this time I had a glimpse of St. Thomas' consistent use of the same logical method with the same spirit of sincerity and integrity—born of an uncompromising devotion to truth; and of his application of this method to the examination of the teaching of the Catholic Church. Apparently he had found no want of harmony between reason and Faith. This made me realize that I could no longer despise the Catholic Faith as, without ever having studied it, I had unconsciously done until this time. I did not believe that St. Thomas' sincere, intelligent and eminently disciplined mind, which had surmounted passion and prejudice to attain a pre-eminent knowledge of philosophic truth, would fall a ready victim to error. In judging of Revelation— of whether God had made known to men certain things concerning Himself—no mind could be better equipped with the understanding of the pertinent criteria of truth than St. Thomas'. This esteem for St. Thomas, I found confirmed by the respect in which he was held by the best thinkers with whom I had come into contact: Herbert, Dr. Mortimer Adler, Dean Richard McKeon, President Robert M. Hutchins.

(13)

At this time I realized that the Catholic Church alone laid claim to possessing the whole religious truth, that it alone claimed an infallible teaching authority. When Dr. Adler, himself said, in comparing the different religious faiths, that the Catholic Faith was the most complete, I understood what he meant; I also understood the so-called dogmatism of the Catholic religion. Knowing that, in the natural order, eternal, changeless truth existed, and that in attaining to it, one must reject as erroneous all that was contradictory to it, I readily understood that if in the supernatural order religious truth existed, the authority to which it was entrusted would be obliged to deny all contradictory opinions as erroneous. That is, a religious society which has Divine truth, must claim that everything which contradicts its doctrine is erroneous, and that every other faith which omits part of its teaching is incomplete. Otherwise it does not really believe that it has the truth, and that all parts of its doctrine are equally true. Likewise, I had come to realize that the word "catholic" means "universal." The Church held its Faith to be objectively true and therefore true for all. The Protestants were divided into hundreds of disagreeing sects, the Jewish religion laid no claim to be other than a religion for Jews, while the Catholic Church proposed its religion as *the* single Divine religion and it invited all equally to accept it.

I had up to this time the modern prejudice against mystery and faith. Certain of the mysteries, such as transubstantiation, had stunned me. How, I thought, can reasonable men or women believe this? I now realized that though my reason was stunned, yet it had nothing to say in contradiction. I had discovered also, in reading Plato, that to be stunned is the first step from deeply imbedded prejudice to true enlightenment. I could see that, logically, the Catholic Faith was invulnerable; it was proposed on the authority of God Who could neither deceive nor be deceived. If this body of

propositions were truly God's word, then it followed that
every proposition would be equally and divinely true. The
Catholic Church, then, would be that secure teacher, which
could lead men through the confusion of passions, prejudice,
self-interest, imperfect reasoning, to the most firm and
secure certitude, based on God's own word. Finally, as Dr.
Adler remarked, any individual who accepted the Divine
authority of this body of truth and then disagreed with some
part of it, would contradict himself, and his private judgement would be an act of pride: would be heresy.

Reformers like Henry VIII and Luther, bore out this view.
It was force of circumstances which carried them out of the
Catholic Church. Likewise, it was clear to me that however
individual Catholics might conduct themselves, the Catholic
Faith itself, if it had Divine authority, would be no less true.
It was the deficiencies of Henry VIII and Luther which set
them against the Catholic Faith (which is not to deny the
abuses in the Catholic Church of his time to which Luther
reacted); likewise other Catholics, who do not go so far, set
themselves against the Faith by not living in accordance with
its precepts.

*"Heresy", according to Catholic teaching, does not pertain
to those who are born into a particular tradition or who
embrace it in good faith, no matter how that tradition
originated. Moreover, historical argumentation is not
important to the quest for Christian unity. Rather, as John
XXIII (who incidentally was a professional historian) said:
"We do not want to prove who was right or wrong. The blame
is on both sides. All we want is to say, 'Let us come together.
Let us make an end of our division.'"*

(14)

My interests now extended to the moral order. At one time
I accepted the behavioristic doctrine, then current, which
denied the existence of the will and of freedom of choice.

In my earlier life I had much difficulty in controlling
disorderly inclinations. I had experienced a lack of freedom
within myself. In my first study of philosophy in Berlin I had

learned that interior liberty presupposed knowledge, since the man who is ignorant is not free to choose or refuse what he does not know. Now, in Chicago, as my knowledge of Divine things and the moral order became more clear, I also found it increasingly easy to conduct myself consistently with my inner convictions and desires, which also were clearer. Hence my experience in that earlier time was in accord with the behavioristic doctrine which I then professed, while now it bore witness to the will and its freedom which true philosophy asserts.

Thanks to my early religious training and especially to my parents, I had always had some moral sense. I was very fortunate in having upright parents with a strong sense of honesty, of fidelity to obligations, love of country, love of race, etc. I also had a sister, five years older than myself, whose selflessness, courage and dedication to others has always been an inspiration to me. Thus I had formed good habits in my early life which were of great assistance. However, I had no reasoned convictions to support these good habits or to strengthen me to withstand the allurements and viewpoints with which I came in contact later. Thus, when I had met the attacks of Voltaire against a "personal" God, Who directed all the events of the universe, I thought his arguments very clever and I adopted a mocking attitude towards religion and even denied the existence of God. Thereafter I settled down to the common belief that if there was a God, I did not know enough to assert his existence. Likewise, when I read of the materialistic theory that sexual relations were as natural as eating and in both cases it was merely necessary to avoid excess, I accepted this as true. It was only a few years later when a person whose judgement and character I respected manifested a different opinion that I changed my mind. This person had shown a violent disgust at the evidence of such laxity. My "innate" moral sense, which I hardly realized existed, heartily approved this reaction. Later I understood that the mean of a virtue is not necessarily a mean with respect to quantity (a moderation in quantity) but may be a mean through due regard to the pertinent circumstances; it is unnatural and unreasonable, for example, to seek the pleasure attached to a natural function while precluding the achievement of the function. In regard to sex, the end of the biological function is the procreation of children; an essential circumstance whose fulfillment reason requires, is this, that the exercise of this function take place in the marriage state.

Erroneous teaching with regard to the control of thoughts and desires also had misled me up to this time. Thus I had the false notion that it was dangerous to put away undesirable thoughts and desires—that "repressions" were thus formed. At this time I did not understand the distinction which psychiatry makes between suppression and repression. The calm, deliberate exclusion of unreasonable thoughts and desires is essential to mental health; this is suppression, not "repression." Oscar Wilde's maxim, which had previously appealed to me as very witty and true, that the only way to get rid of a temptation is to yield to it, had shown itself in my experience to be very poor counsel. On the contrary I had discovered that temptations, yielded to, become very severe masters which exact increasing homage, and that to be really free one must despise and cast them out at once.

Nonetheless, although I thus discovered that I had an innate moral sense and that it was extremely valuable, I had not received in my education any reasoned support for it until my philosophical studies in Chicago.

At this time in addition to discovering that reason alone sufficed to prove the existence of God, the creation of the world, and of the human race, and the existence in each man of an immaterial, immortal soul, root of his reason and will, I discovered that the moral order was a reality, discernible by reason. I learned that the Ten Commandments express the natural moral law. For at the root of human nature is the fundamental desire to seek happiness, to do good and to avoid evil, and in the intelligence are the germinal ideas of those things which are good and those things which are evil. This is the natural moral law, expressed by the Ten Commandments. These latter state the outstanding instances in the classes of things good and evil, as for example the commandment not to kill states the most striking instance of doing bodily injury to oneself or another. I had never previously received such an explanation of the natural moral law and of the Decalogue which expresses it. In my high school and early college years I would perhaps have denied it. Yet my experience had shown me that I did have a moral sense, and this moral sense was evidence of these germinal moral ideas in the intelligence, which false and contrary reasoning had obscured in my mind, but had not radically destroyed.

(15)

The next question that made a deep impression on me in my study of ethics was this: in what does happiness consist? Indeed, this is a question which everyone answers in a practical way since each has, as the goal and ultimate end of all his strivings, his happiness, such as he conceives it to be. Certainly human happiness cannot consist in the external things that merely minister to the body, such as food and clothing, nor in wealth, nor in honors, nor in the esteem and friendship of persons; it cannot consist in pleasure, for often the love of pleasure is itself opposed to happiness. One cannot satisfy the whole person by satisfying a part, such as the body and the interests of the body; the satisfaction of the appetite is often opposed to health as in the case of the glutton. It cannot consist in knowledge; at this time when I was discovering true knowledge, I recognized that it was not sufficient. In what, then, does true and perfect happiness consist? If not in finite and limited creatures, then only in the Infinite and boundless God—Who, I now realized, alone constituted our true end, happiness and perfect completion.

My notion of virtue was now also becoming clearer. Previously this word held for me the ring of meaningless respectability, something which reasonable persons would laugh at. Now I saw that it had real meaning. Virtue is power, the power to obtain happiness. It means, I saw, human, voluntary effort. The one who trembles in battle but yet stays at his post may be exercising the virtue of courage to a higher degree in withstanding his fear and doing his duty than the one who fights without the slightest timidity. It is the voluntary effort which counts.

Where does virtue come from? I was very much impressed by Aristotle's discussion of this question. He proposed the logical possibilities. One of them is that it is acquired through repeated acts forming the habit. This occurs in the formation of acquired virtues. But another source of virtue, according to his illuminated mind, is in God's direct gift: virtue may be the gift of God. He said that the discussion of this possibility belongs not to ethics but to "first" philosophy, that is, to natural theology.

This was my first introduction to anything approaching the concept of grace. The notion of grace appeared later in one of Herbert's courses in esthetics which I was attending. In discussing the neo-Platonist, Plotinus, he explained that for him happiness consisted in contemplating God. How different, he said, was this contemplation of God from the Christian's. For Plotinus, this contemplation was the fruit of human effort and could only be achieved by the intellectual. For the Christian it was the gift of God not restricted to the learned. Christian humility and the equality of men (intellectual or not intellectual) before God, appealed to me.

(16)

During this period at Chicago, despite the development of my knowledge, my external life was very much the same. I was studying philosophy with Professor McKeon and I had begun a survey of medical theory. I was attending certain classes of Herbert's, Dr. Adler's and Dr. Hutchins', and at the social gatherings at Herbert's I frequently met with other students who had similar interests. While this new and promising educational program which was seeking to give true philosophy and the knowledge of God their appropriate pre-eminence interested me deeply, I began to realize its insufficiency. Through true philosophy I had corrected certain of the peculiar ideas of modern godless and unphilosophic education, such as: atheism, agnosticism and religious indifference; skepticism, subjectivism and other peculiarities regarding logic and metaphysics; the theory of extreme evolution; the materialism which denies spiritual realities such as the soul and its powers of reason and the will; unmorality, the want of recognition of objective good and evil and the responsibility of man to do good and to avoid evil in order to attain his true end and happiness, God. I also regarded philosophy as an instrument for the unification and co-ordination of scientific knowledge and for the formulation of crucial experimental projects which would obtain the data necessary to fill in the important gaps in scientific information and understanding. Just as the great scientists of the past had been led to great experiments by systematic, even philosophic reasoning, a group of modern scientists, trained in philosophy, could, I believed, accomplish much. Their discoveries would dispose the scientific world to the acceptance of philosophy and would secure for it its proper place in modern education.

Yet despite all the benefits which could be bestowed by philosophy and by an educational program illuminated by it, the fulfillment of the promise inherent in these benefits would remain outside the power of philosophy. Philosophy could lead to the intellectual knowledge of God and consequently to an ordered understanding of the universe and man. Yet it could not make Him a practical reality. Ethics could furnish an intellectual knowledge of happiness, but it could not provide a man with the means to attain it. I was seeking happiness and something was wanting; my quest for the end of life had not been fulfilled.

(17)

It was at this time that Herbert again directed me by his words and example to the goal I was seeking. He, like myself, had come to Chicago with enthusiasm, glad to be united with others of the same mind as himself. He, too, was not satisfied. He had seen his end with practical clarity and he had bridged the gap; God was an intellectual but also a practical reality to him: the supreme good, supremely worth striving after. He knew, and said, that he had not arrived at the truth through his own power; it was God's work. He was grateful to God and wished to do something for Him. This spirit of honesty and his uncompromising determination to "follow through" and to be true to the light which he received evoked my profound respect. This was in conformity with my own desire.

There were obstacles to "following through." God's work was not unopposed in us. In Herbert, I discerned now a more deliberate and courageous effort at self-discipline. He wanted to be generous, to make a return to God. He expressed his detestation of worldliness—the spirit of compromise. He did not hesitate to expose in his friends the motives which were preventing them from being true to their inner convictions (he did this in my case, as I shall gratefully recall in a moment). However, he spoke with such clarity and with such obvious love for his friends that those whom he thus singled out were rather led to seek his guidance than to be offended. He gave what advice he could. Here, too, his honesty was manifest: guidance, he said, was to be looked for from qualified persons, experts in guidance; he was not an expert; the experts in guidance were the Catholic priests.

Herbert disclosed to me my ambitions for knowledge and alternations from humility to arrogance. His statements made my weaknesses clearer to me. I felt a firmer determination than ever before to overcome my defects.

On one occasion, in the midst of my anxieties I turned to the New Testament—for the first time—and happened upon a passage which brought a sudden great peace of mind. It was this: (Luke 12:22–31): [1]

---

[1]. New Testament quotations are from the Confraternity of Christian Doctrine edition of the New Testament. Old Testament quotations are from the Douay version. The Douay is the version that was available to me at the time of my conversion. At this time, I frequently consulted a Jewish Bible to check on the texts of the prophets, rather than relying simply on a Christian version of the Old Testament.

But He said to His disciples: "Therefore I say to you, do not be anxious for your life, what you shall eat; nor yet for your body, what you shall put on. The life is a greater thing than the food, and the body than the clothing. Consider the ravens; they neither sow nor reap, they have neither storeroom nor barn; yet God feeds them. Of how much more value are you than they! But which of you by being anxious about it can add to his stature a single cubit? Therefore if you are not able to do even a very little thing, why are you anxious concerning the rest?

"See how the lilies grow; they neither toil nor spin, yet I say to you that not even Solomon in all his glory was arrayed like one of these. But if God so clothes the grass which today is alive in the field and tomorrow is thrown into the oven, how much more you, O you of little faith!

"And as for you, do not seek what you shall eat, or what you shall drink; and do not exalt yourselves (for after all these things the nations of the world seek): but your Father knows that you need these things. But seek the kingdom of God, and all these things shall be given you besides."

From this passage I gained a clearer insight into God's Providence and His love for men. His condition, seek first the kingdom of God and His justice, made a deep impression on my mind, as also did the gentle reproach: "O you of little faith." These words of Jesus Christ were the first words of the New Testament which I had read for myself. Through them I conceived of God more perfectly than I had ever done before. God was a Father. He proposed to man a kingdom to be sought before all else. Not necessarily in the order of execution—i.e., in the means adopted—for support of one's bodily life could easily be the first means taken in the seeking of this kingdom; but first in the order of intention—first as the end of all one's human activity. I understood also that if God cared so splendidly for the lilies of the field, how much more wonderful must be his care for His children—for men and women. To deserve His care, His condition must be fulfilled—to seek the kingdom of God. Anxieties about temporal matters must not so preoccupy the heart as to prevent the seeking of God's kingdom. Philosophy had shown me God as he could be known by reason. But here I experienced a simple revelation of God from God's own viewpoint—beautiful, luminous yet mysterious, harmonious with reason and experience, convincing, enlightening and

directing human effort, promising in divine words Divine
help. In trusting Him I had experienced great peace.

Herbert's example had shown me the goodness of being
grateful and devoted to God as to a Person really existing,
powerful to make men happy, Who could be sought and
served. However, my conduct and interior life did not
change notably. Herbert, then desirous for my perfection,
which was not to be found in myself, said: "I have no faith in
you." I realized Herbert was in a rare, black mood when he
said this. But I did not think that this perception should
prevent me from taking his words seriously. They shook me
deeply.

As I considered this, my attitude towards myself became
more clear. Did I have faith in myself? I knew myself, now,
to be moved from time to time by ambition, vanity, pride,
insincerity. Towards what was I moving? I knew also, on the
other hand, that I had been striving to become better, and it
seemed to me that this was my principal endeavor.

Yet the great question remained: in what would I place my
ultimate end? In myself, my selfish interests and desires and
views? Against this, I firmly resolved. Herbert's censure had
aroused me from my torpor, and I resolved to seek God
sincerely, in simplicity and in truth. Having so resolved, I felt
a conviction of my sincerity and correspondence with the
condition God asked of me, and peace returned.

I now felt free from a servile dependence on the approval
of others. But I determined not to deceive myself. I resolved
to employ appropriate means: prayer and the daily reading of
the Gospels.

CHAPTER THREE

GOD'S KINGDOM: FRIENDSHIP WITH
GOD THROUGH FAITH IN
THE GODHEAD OF
JESUS CHRIST

(1) God takes me up the spiritual mountain.

(2) The Name of Jesus.

(3) The Gospel of Jesus Christ; "Who do you say that I am?"

(4) My question is likewise answered; His authority is from God, His Father; He is true God.

(5) The Resurrection of Jesus Christ; He passes through the locked door of my heart—I believe in the Godhead of Jesus Christ.

(6) "How sweet is the Lord": the gentleness and loveableness of Jesus; His Revelation is the revelation and sharing of the interior life of God.

(7) His merciful kindness: the gratuitousness of the gift of Faith and of the friendship of God.

(8) The Blessed Trinity; the Word made Flesh is come to win the friendship of men. I saw His glory, the glory of the Only-Begotten of the Father, full of grace and truth.

(9) The life of union with God: God dwells in the heart of the true believer. The validity of Catholic moral principles; the peace of a good conscience.

(10) I determine to be baptized in the Roman Catholic Church.

(1)

It seems to me that in human nature there is a well-nigh infinite longing. I had not been able to satisfy that longing. What was it that would do so? Once, in approaching New York City from a distance I had been struck by the outline of the city. The great cluster of tall buildings glistened like spires in the sunlight, and there was a quiet majesty in the scene, as of a noble city. A similar sense of grandeur, of something above the things of the natural world, impressed me on coming to the top of a mountain and suddenly seeing in a sweeping view the surrounding countryside. These experiences elevated my mind and secretly prophesied: there is a view, majestic, noble, which comprehends all things; one comes upon it suddenly. That I did come upon this grand view, comprehending all things, will be soon evident, for even now, I am relating my progress up the spiritual mountain. Wherever such super-enlightened impressions as these come from (perhaps from our guardian angels), nevertheless they raise the human spirit to hope. It has a longing for the end which it has not seen and which it does not know and which nothing on earth can satisfy; its confidence and hope of arriving at its end is strengthened in just such hidden and secret ways. I mention one more impression of this sort from my youth. It was on a Sunday when the streets in New York City were deserted. I was looking down a great avenue; the high buildings formed a canyon. A storm had just passed over the city, and a great light was pouring out of the heavens and dispelling the darkness, giving the impression that it was breaking through from another world—a world of great light. The things of this world suddenly seemed tiny and small, and time seemed short.

Following my resolution not to allow myself to fall into
self-deception, I determined to act in conformity with the
maxim, "Seek first the kingdom of God"; that is, I was going
to put the pursuit of His kingdom above all else. I wished to
be practical, I wanted my daily activity to reflect this
determination. Herbert had made a suggestion which I had
followed; he had said, "Pray." I did not remember having
prayed since childhood. In those days, when I had doubts
about whether there was a God, and I had a stomach-ache,
the doubts would dissolve and I would turn inwardly to my
God and say very quickly, "Yes, I do believe," and somehow
the pain became endurable. Now, the pain was of a different
sort. I was blind, I knew it. I could not see my end, I could not
see the way. My prayer was very self-conscious. I made it on
my knees. I had the feeling that whatever I was, I was what I
was in God's sight.

Following this, things took a much quicker pace. I had had
a glimpse of God's greatness, of how much His infinity
exceeded the things of earth and of how small and mean
human passions and human strivings were, and my own
self-conscious strivings were quieted. This experience of
God's greatness and the smallness of all else in comparison
was like the sweeping view from the mountain. It was like
the great mass of light pouring into the city canyon after the
storm. God was like the majestic city seen in outline from
afar. Yet certainly, He would be more beautiful as one
approached nearer Him. I began to read the Gospels daily.

At this time there were no real obstacles for me in the
Catholic religion. I had learned that God existed and
suspected that the Catholic Church offered the only true
religion; moreover, as a Jew, I was strongly inclined to
accept the Catholic Church simply because it was the
fulfillment of the Jewish religion and because it had been
founded by the promised Messiah. I had shyly taken up a
book which contained the Apostles' Creed, the creed of the
Catholic Faith, and read it through. I decided there was
nothing contrary to reason or to any of my convictions in it.

But until this time nothing had impelled me to become a Catholic. My life was now much more satisfactory than it had ever been; I was working on a research project which I thought contained great promise; the study of philosophy satisfied my desire for natural truth; my associations at the university were very cordial and my daily life happy. Yet there had crystallized in me the realization that this was not all; that, despite all these things I remained vain, proud and of no great worth. I had an inner conviction of an end which was far greater than the ends promised by my natural activities; I realized this end was God and I resolved to seek Him above all else. In the reading of the Gospels I gradually began to see the promised light coming forth from a world beyond and opening up a way. I enjoyed great peace in reading the Gospels, yet it was a peace sustained by the effort of suppressing old prejudices.

(2)

In my early religious life the name of Jesus Christ had, as I mentioned at the beginning of this story, been associated in my mind with the persecution of the Jewish race. Subconsciously I had, since then, experienced a sense of guilt—as if I were implicated in His death. When I had read in some magazine that it was not the Jews, after all, but Pontius Pilate, the Roman, who had really put Jesus to death, I had been inclined to believe this, with some relief, and had felt that perhaps His death had been attributed to the Jewish race simply out of hatred, just as later it was said that in the Jewish rites the blood of Gentile children was used. Subsequently I had followed the common opinion among the Jewish religious teachers that Jesus was an extremely noble man and that He could be claimed by Jews as a great Jew.

In Chicago I had begun to realize how deeply Jesus was loved by Catholics. I did not at that time explicitly realize the wonderful friendship and sympathy which Catholics, especially Catholics who are truly attached to Jesus, feel towards the Jews. Nonetheless, I had felt this to some extent in my relation with William Gorman, a Catholic, of whom as well as of Herbert Ratner and Herbert Schwartz, I had been a constant friend since Ann Arbor days.

Now, in reading the Gospels, certain of my old prejudices and oversensitiveness remained. In addition to this, the language itself offered some obstacle. There was at times a strangeness of expression. Finally, modern prejudices, which remained imbedded in my mind, rebelled against placing credence in angels, devils and miracles—which were frequently mentioned in the Gospel story. Yet I knew that all these reactions were simply peculiarities arising out of my previous experiences and circumstances, and that they had no basis in reason. Consequently I was resolved to suppress them in order to gain an intelligent and fair impression of the story that was being unfolded. Dr. Hutchins said in an Honors Course on the Great Books, (which I audited at this time) that to make sense of the Bible, it is necessary to read it as if it were true. I did want to see what sense the Bible made. With regard to miracles I now found them not so strange as formerly. It seemed reasonable to me that the Author of nature could, when He had a higher purpose in view, suspend the laws of nature at will.

(3)

As I continued reading the Gospels, I recognized that their story, the account of the life and teaching of Jesus Christ, had the freshness of the testimony of eye-witnesses. Before Jesus had begun to teach, a great Jewish prophet had arisen and won the hearts of the Jewish people. Like his predecessors he promised the coming of the Messiah, but this time there was an exultant note, "The Kingdom of God is at hand." Indeed, one day, John the Baptist, standing by the river Jordan, pointed out the figure of Jesus and said to his disciples, "Behold the lamb of God who takes away the sin of the world." —He, John, who was approved by all as a prophet of God, was not worthy to unloose the shoes of Jesus, he told them.

After this had followed the preaching of Jesus, which, I was surprised to learn, He restricted to the Jews, to whom, He explained, He had been sent. He said to them: "Do not think that I have come to destroy the law or the Prophets. I have not come to destroy but to fulfill." (Matt.5:17) The religion which He had come to institute was not to be the destruction, but the fulfillment of the Jewish religion—of the law and of the prophecies concerning the Messiah.

Jesus at this time announced the path to happiness in the celebrated "Sermon on the Mount." Although I failed to grasp the import of His words, I felt the impression of a real personality, of great authority not presumptuously arrogated, nor delegated by human agency. Whence was it? It seemed intrinsic to Him.

Wherever he went He cured by miracles the diseases of the people, having compassion on them: He gave this outward proof that, although He was not sent to them by the Scribes and Pharisees, the authorities in the Jewish Church, yet He was truly sent by God. As time went on the great question in men's minds became: Who is He? Such had also been the question which His words aroused in me. He allowed men to judge for themselves; they had His teaching, the prophets and His miracles; they had the witness of John the Baptist in whom the people believed.

Two parties had formed: His disciples, men who gave up all they had in order to follow Him and His teaching, and His enemies, the ruling class. One day He placed before His disciples the question which was in the minds of men and women, asking them whom they thought Him to be. Simon answered that some thought He was Elijah, the prophet, others John the Baptist and still others one of the other prophets. Of His disciples He asked, "But who do you say that I am?" Simon Peter said, "Thou art the Christ, the Son of the living God." Jesus' response was instant and uncompromising: "Blessed art thou, Simon Bar-Jona, for flesh and blood has not revealed this to thee, but my Father in heaven. And I say to thee, thou art Peter, and upon this rock I will

build my Church and the gates of hell shall not prevail
against it. And I will give thee the keys of the kingdom of
heaven; and whatever thou shalt bind on earth shall be
bound in heaven, and whatever thou shalt loose on earth
shall be loosed in heaven." (Matt, 16:16)

From this time He had predicted that He would be crucified
and on the third day would arise from the dead.

(4)

In my mind, doubts remained. Perhaps the enmity of the
Jewish religious leaders was based on His desire to form a
new church. Yet He was a perfect observer of the Mosaic
Law even up to the moment of His death: the celebrated Last
Supper began with the observance of the Passover rite, the
offering and eating of the paschal lamb. His enemies had
sought evidence against His fulfillment of the observances of
the Jewish religion, but had found nothing of significance.

Finally the opposition between them came to a head in the
controversies in Jerusalem where Jesus was teaching in the
Temple. In the Gospel story of these controversies I saw
clearly the account of a real occurrence. The writers were
obviously unmoved by passion or prejudice—their work bore
witness to their integrity, sincerity and impartiality. The
characters were not the characters of fiction. Finally, the
words of Jesus had a comprehensive, spontaneous lumino-
sity which did not, it struck me, have a merely human origin.
In these controversies His opponents were always a small
class of the Jews, while the great multitude of the Jews were
in admiration of Jesus and of His manner of answering the
scribes, Pharisees and Sadducees.

At this time this small class, consisting of the chief priests
and elders of the Jewish people, asked Him by what
authority He did these things. Again the question was similar
to the one His words had evoked in my mind. By what
authority did He teach as He did? For He spoke not as the
philosophers, depending on principles evident to reason or
on demonstrations based on such principles, but as if He had
knowledge of Himself. He in His turn announced to them by

a parable that the Divine Authority was now about to be transferred from the Jewish to the Catholic religion, because of their condemnation of the Messiah. Then in confirmation of the truthfulness of this prophecy He quoted the Psalm 117, lines 22 and following, and Isaiah, 28:16:

"Did you never read in the Scriptures,
 'The stone which the builders rejected,
  has become the corner stone;
 'By the Lord this has been done,
  and it is wonderful in our eyes?' "

Then he continued:

"Therefore I say to you, that the kingdom of God will be taken away from you and will be given to a people yielding its fruits. And he who falls on this stone will be broken to pieces; but upon whomever it falls, it will grind him to powder."

And when the chief priests and Pharisees had heard his parables, they knew that he was speaking about them. And though they sought to lay hands on him, they feared the people, because they regarded him as a prophet (Matt.21:23–46).

When the Pharisees came to question Him, Jesus took the offensive. He asked them concerning the expected Messiah, was he to be a mere man, or something greater?

Now while the Pharisees were gathered together, Jesus questioned them, saying, "What do you think of the Christ? Whose son is he?" They said to him, "David's." He said to them, "How then does David in the Spirit call him Lord, saying,
 'The Lord said to my Lord:
 "Sit thou at my right hand,
  till I make thy enemies
   the footstool of thy feet." '
If David, therefore, calls him 'Lord,' how is he his son?" And no one could answer him a word; neither did anyone dare from that day forth to ask him any more questions (Matt.22:41–46).

"The Lord said to my Lord"—David calls the Messiah, who is to be his own lineal descendant, "my Lord." Who then is the "Lord" who speaks thus to David's Lord? The Lord our God, we know, is One. Who else, then, but the Father, Who

speaks thus to His Son, the Christ, Who is One with Him? His
enemies dared not from that day to question Him further.
Their query, "By what authority dost thou do these things?
And who gave thee this authority?" was now answered. So
likewise was my question concerning the authority by which
He spoke as He did—an authority which did not seem to be
presumptuously assumed, which was not delegated by any
human agency, but which seemed naturally resident in His
very Personality. The answer was the answer Simon Peter
had given. His authority arose from His Person and from His
Father. He was the Christ, the Son of the living God. His
authority was resident in His very Personality. He was God. I
determined to put aside my doubts, and accept with a quiet
and receptive mind, the great truth which had thus won my
assent. I was not willing to be among His enemies.

This conflict seemed real to me. I could identify the people
on both sides with types I knew in real life. I felt that one had
to take one side or the other. Indifference or neutrality did
not seem possible for me.

Some time after this had followed the crucifixion. The High
Priest called Him a blasphemer, making Himself God. Was He
a blasphemer? Certainly He was a man and certainly no mere
man could be God unless He had in addition to His human
nature the Divine Nature.

By my birth I had been associated in a certain way with the
Scribes and Pharisees, having inherited their antagonism to
Jesus—Otherwise why was I not a Catholic from my earliest
years? The Catholic Church was simply the Jewish religion
fulfilled by the great Messiah come to His people. He had
formed a church founded on the twelve Apostles and a
multitude of the Jews of that day. Why was I not among their
descendants?

On the question, what think you of Christ? I had had from
my early days a pre-judgment. For I had had no doubt that
He was not God. However, the succession of events which I
have been recounting had brought me to the reading of the
Gospels with an open mind and with a certain understanding
of the basic truths underlying Christ's teaching and Person.

Having my choice between His disciples and His enemies, I placed myself in the former class. No, He was not a blasphemer. I felt in accord with Nicodemus the Pharisee who, coming to Him at night to speak with him, had said, "Rabbi, we know that thou hast come a teacher from God, for no one can work these signs that thou workest unless God be with Him." (John 3:2).

(5)

Three days after Christ's death His tomb was found open and empty. An angel in shining white garments with a countenance like lightning said to the loyal women who had come to finish the ceremonial annointing of His Body, "Why do you seek the living among the dead? He is not here, but has risen." Then He had entered the room in which His apostles were gathered behind locked doors, passing through the door. This seemed very strange; I read on. After a growing acquaintance with the story of Jesus, I came to this passage again. Now I accepted the account without hesitancy—I had begun to believe in the Godhead of Jesus Christ! This is what I read:

When it was late that same day, the first of the week, though the doors where the disciples gathered had been closed for fear of the Jews, Jesus came and stood in the midst and said to them, "Peace be to you!" And when he had said this, he showed them his hands and his side. The disciples therefore rejoiced at the sight of the Lord. He therefore said to them again, "Peace be to you! as the Father has sent me, I also send you." When he had said this, he breathed upon them and said to them, "Receive the Holy Spirit; whose sins you shall forgive, they are forgiven them; and whose sins you shall retain, they are retained."

Now Thomas, one of the Twelve, called the Twin, was not with them when Jesus came. The other disciples therefore said to him, "We have seen the Lord." But he said to them, "Unless I see in his hands the print of the nails, and put my hand into his side, I will not believe."

And after eight days, his disciples were again inside, and Thomas with them. Jesus came, the doors being closed, and stood in their midst, and said, "Peace be to you!" Then he said to Thomas, "Bring here thy finger, and see my hands; and bring here thy hand and put it into my side; and be not unbelieving, but believing." Thomas answered and said to him, "My Lord and my God!" Jesus said to him, "Because thou hast seen me, thou hast believed. Blessed are they who have not seen, and yet have believed" (John 20:19–29).

Indeed a great change had taken place since I had read of the Resurrection the first time. The doors of my heart had been shut and locked but now Christ had passed through them. I was now truly His disciple.

(6)

Now I began to see "How sweet is the Lord," I had been over-sensitive in reading the Gospels at first, and the gentleness and lovableness of Jesus had not shown forth from the text. His great compassion for the Jewish people, who reciprocated it with loving admiration, His tears for the widow of Naim whom He met on the way to bury her son, and his going about the country healing every sickness, had not stood out so clearly in my mind. Instead of this I was struck by His outspoken expressions, towards the end of His public life, against the Scribes and Pharisees, whom He called hypocrites, liars and vipers. These expressions had stung me. I knew, however, that they were not His way of addressing His opponents generally, nor the Jews in particular, nor did they apply to the Jews of the present day. They were spoken to men who had seen His miracles, heard His words and had proof of the truthfulness of His mission and of His authority and yet were determined for their own personal advantage to put Him to death.

Their guilt in the death of Jesus Christ follows from this, that they personally judged Him worthy of death, although they, learned in the Hebrew Scriptures, had sufficient means for knowing of His innocence and of the truthfulness of His claim to be Christ the Messiah. Needless to say, then, I was mistaken in feeling that any actual guilt fell upon me as a possible descendant of these Jews. Even the Jews who dwelt in foreign lands and were not present in Jerusalem at this time (the Jews of the Dispersion) were innocent of the death of Jesus Christ. On the other hand, taking the idea of responsibility in a sense wider than personal actual responsibility, not only the Jews but the Gentiles—in the person of the Roman Governor, Pontius Pilate, who condemned Jesus to the death of the Cross—were responsible for His death, so that the true cause of His death—the sins of all men—might be more manifest. For He came to lay down His life as a ransom for all men, that all might, by Faith and Baptism in His Name, come to the knowledge and love of God, in which is eternal life.

Yet, merely because I was of the Jewish race, the words of Jesus, spoken without rancor and for the welfare of those whom He so characterized, had rankled. Nor had they seemed, at first, to fit in with my conception of the ideal man: the man of gentleness and love towards all. Yet He Who spoke thus was the same Jesus Who at the moment of His crucifixion, thought first of all of obtaining forgiveness for His enemies and executioners, saying, "Father, forgive them, for they know not what they do."

I had not foreseen the union of justice and mercy, when I had conceived my ideal of a man. But in Jesus justice knew the wickedness of His enemies, and for their good declared it, while mercy desired the suspension of the punishment due them on the condition that they admit their faults and repent.

But now that Jesus had passed by faith through the doors of my heart, I began to learn the depth of His Goodness. This was revealed to me in such passages of Saint John's Gospel as the following (John 10:7–18):

Again, therefore, Jesus said to them, "Amen, amen, I say to you, I am the door of the sheep. . . . If anyone enter by me he shall be safe, and shall go in and out, and shall find pastures. . . . I came that they may have life, and have it more abundantly.

"I am the good shepherd. The good shepherd lays down his life for his sheep. . . . I know mine and mine know me, even as the Father knows me and I know the Father; and I lay down my life for my sheep. And other sheep I have that are not of this fold. Them also I must bring, and they shall hear my voice, and there shall be one fold and one shepherd. For this reason the Father loves me, because I lay down my life that I may take it up again. No one takes it from me, but I lay it down of myself. I have the power to lay it down, and I have the power to take it up again. Such is the command I have received from my Father.''

But particularly in His Farewell Discourse was His great love disclosed. Here He was speaking to those of His race who had given up their associations and their former mode of life in order to share His life. These were His disciples and His apostles who were to carry His Name, His teaching and His way of life to all the nations and all the peoples of the globe, even to the end of time, as He predicted. To them and to all those who, through them, would believe in Him, even down to the present day, He said, (John 15:9–15):

"As the Father has loved me, I also have loved you. Abide in my love. If you keep my commandments you will abide in my love, as I also have kept my Father's commandments, and abide in his love. These things I have spoken to you that my joy may be in you, and that your joy may be made full.

"This is my commandment, that you love one another as I have loved you. Greater love than this no one has, that one lay down his life for his friends. You are my friends if you do the things I command you. No longer do I call you servants, because the servant does not know what his master does. But I have called you friends, because all things that I have heard from my Father I have made known to you."

Here is revealed the friendship of God for men and women and His goodness in confiding to them, through Jesus Christ, secrets—such as were hidden from the philosophers—of His own interior Life and purposes.

(7)

I now began to realize the kindness with which God had treated me. When I had re-read the story of the resurrection, I had an inner realization of its truth. This realization had not come from the natural light of reason, for I could not with perfect certitude assert that the text I was reading was what it claimed to be—an historical account; I could not assert that it was true from the nature of the event—for the resurrection itself presents a difficulty to the natural reason: it is not in the order of nature that the dead rise to life. Whence, then, came this certainty? Not from my emotions, for up to this time I had had no affection for Christ; He had not met with my idea of what a perfect man should be, but had aroused some resentment and antagonism in me. This inner certainty, clear and evident, full of peace, corresponded entirely with what I had previously learned Divine Faith to be—a gift of God by which human reason is supernaturally enlightened to see the truthfulness of what is beyond its natural capacity to know and in which the will is drawn to adhere joyfully to this truth. And indeed, from this time the thought of Christ, and of the Divine order which He had brought into the world, was accompanied by joy.

Now I saw how personally God had spoken to me, for to me were addressed these words: "No longer do I call you servants, because the servant does not know what his master does. But I have called you friends, because all things that I have heard from my Father I have made known to you." God personally loved me; in these words He was telling me so. He had befriended me and this at a time when I clearly saw how unworthy I was even of the friendship of men. But God, in choosing His friends, is not hindered by their unworthiness, for who is worthy to be the friend of God? It is His choice and His love which render a man worthy. He had given me the gift of Faith.

(8)

The doctrine of the Trinity, that God is a substance, one in nature and three in person, presented no difficulty to me. In my studies of philosophy and my acquaintance with theology, I had come to understand that the doctrine contained nothing contrary to reason. A human person, knowing himself, would have an imperfect knowledge which, nonetheless, would bear some resemblance to himself. He might have a certain esteem or respect or love for himself as being, for example, honest and sincere. In a Divine person, however, the knowledge of Himself could not be imperfect but perfect, and if it were perfect, it would be identical with its object. The knowledge of God would then be God Himself.

This is what Christ and the Catholic Church teach; the Second Person of the Blessed Trinity proceeds from God the Father, begotten in that act by which He knows Himself. Similarly, God the Father and God the Son in looking upon each other, in seeing that They are one identical nature, one God, beautiful in every respect, love each other with a most perfect love, and this love is God, existing always. God the Holy Ghost proceeds from God the Father and God the Son by way of their love for each other. This the Gospels and the Church likewise teach. This doctrine of the Trinity of God was foreshadowed in the Old Testament. That it is not an impossibility, reason can assert (as the exposition just given shows). This doctrine I found most appealingly presented in the Gospel story itself. Who but the Son, the Word made flesh, descending to men by taking a human nature, conversing with them in sacred friendship, could make known this intimate truth concerning His own interior life? Indeed, for this He became man, suffered and died; atoning for man's sin that He might disclose to them His own mystery and make them truly His friends. And this message He confided to them for transmission to all who through them would believe in Him, instituting for this purpose the rock of the Papacy in Simon Peter. He assured Peter of this measure of success in his mission: the gates of hell should not prevail against him. He would always have a living successor keeping intact the Divine Truth which the Son of God had brought to the earth, for the winning of friends among men. When I read the following verses, then, in Saint John (John 1:1–14), I understood them:

> IN THE BEGINNING was the Word,
>   and the Word was with God;
>   and the Word was God.
> He was in the beginning with God.
> All things were made through him,
>   and without him was made
>   nothing that has been made.
> In him was life,
>   and the life was the light of men.

And the light shines in the darkness;
   and the darkness grasped it not.
There was a man,
one sent from God,
whose name was John.
This man came as a witness,
   to bear witness concerning the light,
   that all might believe through him.
He was not himself the light,
   but was to bear witness to the light.
It was the true light
   that enlightens every man
   who comes into the world.
He was in the world,
   and the world was made through him,
   and the world knew him not.
He came unto his own,
   and his own received him not.
But to as many as received him
   he gave the power of becoming sons of God;
   to those who believe in his name:
Who were born not of blood,
   nor of the will of the flesh,
   nor of the will of man,
   but of God.
And the Word was made flesh,
   and dwelt among us.
And we saw his glory—
   glory as of the only-begotten of the Father—
   full of grace and of truth.

(9)

What had previously been merely an intellectual reality now was a personal Friend with Whom direct conversation (prayer) was possible, and this through His most merciful and generous gift of Faith. I had found a wonderful harmony among true science, perennial philosophy and Catholic theology. In the Gospels, whose authenticity was for me sufficiently attested by their contents, I had glimpsed the superhuman, the divine Personality and authority of Christ, Whose teaching was the source of Catholic theology and the subject matter of its faith. Through the gift of Faith I had better appreciated His lovableness; and this gift itself I found to be a witness to its own reality and power, and to the reality of the God Who through it had come to dwell in my heart.

Now I could better understand practical morality, the condition for a life of union with God. Up to this time I had been reading the Gospels and St. Augustine's explanation of St. John's Gospel. Now I came across a manual for Jesuit seminarians and read it. In it I found rules of conduct and psychological and moral principles which were of great help.

Just as I had previously scoffed at everything which smacked of piety or devotion as if it were based on sentimentality and in disagreement with reason, so I had treated sin and evil as if non-existent. Yet I had not been unaware of the disorder within me, just as every person who has moments of honesty recognizes disorder in himself. I had begun to learn the names of some of these disorderly inclinations: pride, an "excitement" about oneself; vanity, an exaggerated desire for the approval or esteem of others, etc., etc. Even before I began to read the New Testament I realized that my pride was turning me away from seeing clearly my own defects, and consequently from governing my actions and my emotions in accordance with my convictions. I also began to realize that at times I acted against my convictions notwithstanding the realization at the moment that I was doing so. This is sin. I was learning to examine my conscience. I discovered that the headaches and many other difficulties I had been subject to arose from vanity and pride and that I could forestall these inclinations and regulate my interior. I learned now the common-sense doctrine of foreseeing and of avoiding the occasions in which such objectionable emotions are aroused, or guarding against objectionable emotions when such occasions were unavoidable. The rules and principles in the Jesuit manual thus helped me considerably. These rules were applied in a special way to govern the association of the sexes.

This experience of an integration of character through the understanding and application of Catholic moral principles served as a practical proof of their validity. I realized that the things which Catholic morality calls evil are really evil, disturbing one's ability to act in accord with one's convictions and disturbing the mind, heart, and body. I also saw that only through acting in accordance with these moral principles and by the help of God's grace was it possible to maintain consistency in conduct and true peacefulness of mind and heart. Thus did I prove, besides the validity of Catholic moral principles, their superiority to various psychiatric theories and methods. Indeed, the entire range of my education, scientific, medical, social, philosophic, had not provided such clear and true principles, such helpful practical rules for the integration of personal life and activity and for consistency in conduct. In Aristotle's *Ethics* I indeed had met with many of these principles, for many are possessed by true philosophy. Yet it was my knowledge of the divinity of Jesus Christ and of God's love for me which most powerfully helped me in these matters. This knowledge inspired me with trust in God and with true peace. It disposed me to humbly and truthfully identify and acknowledge my sins and deficiencies. It led me to realize that my evil inclinations could be corrected, could be supplanted by good inclinations in harmony with my good convictions and resolutions. This hope was supported by the experience of God's grace helping me thus to amend my life.

Until this time I had had a certain leaning on the approval of others whose special sincerity and insight had attracted me. I felt, for example, that Herbert had a vision of the end and the way, which I lacked; therefore I was dependent on his judgment. I realized this dependency when I experienced how shaken I had been by Herbert's words: "I have no faith in you!" A change had occurred when I put into practice the principle, "Seek first the Kingdom of God and His Justice," for I knew that to do this sincerely and with one's whole heart was the highest rule one could follow, and I was able to judge by myself, in the light of this principle, independently of Herbert's approval. I knew that if Herbert saw my resolutions and what I was doing to carry them out, he would be satisfied (otherwise he would not be worthy of my confidence). I was determined that from this time on I would not allow the undue seeking of the approval of others, or pride in what I was doing, to contaminate the motive that was directing me. Therefore, I made no mention of the reading that I was doing or of the interior growth that was taking place. I was at peace, with a peace springing from an inner certainty. God himself was now my guide. This was the peace and certainty of a good conscience, which God alone can effect.

(10)

The day came when I confided to Herbert that I believed. "However," I went on, "from time to time my faith seems to waver and that gives me concern because I know that faith is steadfast." Herbert's expression was one of sweetness and great peace. "Peter," he said, "was not steadfast until he was baptized with the Holy Spirit." At that moment I saw that one thing was wanting to me, baptism. With great joy, I determined to be baptized!

Shortly thereafter I visited Father Gillis, Paulist Father, in New York City. The summer vacation had begun. After a short conversation, I told him that I was sailing for Europe that week, and would like to be baptized before I left. Father gave me some books to read and told me to come back after my trip to Europe. This was my first meeting with a priest of the Roman Catholic Church. In him, I found what I have experienced with many others: cordiality and a charming respect for the individuality and liberty of others. Jesus Christ lives in His priests!

CHAPTER FOUR

GOD'S KINGDOM: JESUS CHRIST AND THE ROMAN CATHOLIC CHURCH —ONE BODY

"I am the Way, the Truth and the Life"

(1) Traveling in Europe—"Blessed are the poor in spirit."

(2) Traveling to the kingly city of God.

(3) Our first parents; Adam and Eve; the Fall.

(4) Its consequences: explanation of evil.

(5) The Redeemer comes.

(6) The Particular and Final Judgments.

(7) Mankind without a covenant, and under the old Covenant; the New Covenant: the Catholic Church is the Kingdom of God, Triumphant—in Heaven, Militant—on earth.

(8) The greatness of the Jewish race is extolled by Catholic doctrine.

(9) The way to the heavenly city; I prepare for baptism—incorporation into the Mystical Body of Christ—the Church; divine character of the Church.

(10) Justice comes not through Communism, but through Christ. The ideal of Communism is anarchy: an impossible society, without God. The way of Communism is perpetual bloody revolution—the extermination of men. The ideal of the Church is Jesus Christ. The Way is Baptism which requires Faith in the Divinity of Christ and renunciation of internal disorder—the extermination of sin. Justice—the justification of the internal as well as of external life—comes through Jesus Christ.

(1)

That summer I was sitting on the balcony of an Italian hotel overlooking Lake Maggiore. The sky was clear with a beautiful pale blue tint. The mountains surrounding the lake were visible in detail conveying the impression that no medium existed between them and the spectator. Uncle Ben had ordered breakfast. He said, "I am trying to show you how a millionaire lives." I had seen how a millionaire lived, but also how a millionaire thought and felt. On the French Line steamship, the *Normandie*, I had met many men and women who were frequently very tired, seemed to feel very empty and had missed the point of life. Their children, young men and women, were still young enough to hunger for something beyond. They had, however, begun to follow in the tracks of their parents. These people who took elaborate means to seek relief from their cares and troubles were certainly not happy. Jesus had said, "Blessed are the poor in spirit."

For my part I had enjoyed eating giant snails, which tasted like meaty mushrooms, and found the *Normandie* a very comfortable boat. This trip was made more pleasant by the company of my teen-age, intelligent and innocent cousin Janet, and my gracious Aunt Aurene. At Venice I had enjoyed sightseeing in a gondola with an acquaintance from our hotel, a young woman, who was also in Venice for the first time. At the hotel itself I had had a great deal of fun with some English friends with whom I always took tea before retiring. Yet the enjoyment was superficial, and was followed by fatigue and boredom. My true happiness and peace, deep, substantial, I found in the retirement of my heart, in the contemplation of Divine truths.

In contrast to my present surroundings were those of the University of Chicago. Bill's room, for example. He had a room in back of "Grandma's" house, as the boys called their

landlady. It was small and square. Around its yellow walls
Bill had placed small postcard size reproductions of Fra
Angelico's paintings. Here he sat, smoking his pipe and
studying St. Thomas' tracts with great contentment. "For
my part," he had said one day on returning from the richly
furnished home of a fellow-student, "I would be content
with this room for the rest of my life." No one who knew Bill
could doubt that he meant it. "For my part," I had thought,
"I can see how attracted I am by worldly distinctions and
riches." I felt my carnality in contrast to Bill's spirituality.
On another occasion in Chicago, we were having dinner
together, near a table occupied by two ladies and a
gentleman. One couple were obviously husband and wife.
Both were fashionably dressed; she wore jewels. Their chests
were thrown out in that attitude often seen in those who
have "found their place" in the world. The other lady was
small, modestly and poorly dressed, but with a sweet and
lovely countenance. She was listening graciously. Bill had
expressed his love for the poor. I realized how foolish was my
love for the rich. Certainly the poor in spirit, like Bill, like
this poor little lady, undoubtedly poor from birth, had the
better part. Bill's peace and joy were deeply rooted in his
heart, and were not to be disturbed by changes in circumstances, in position, by humiliations. His peace was not
disturbed by restless desires for honor, distinction or riches.
If he remained faithful to the part he had chosen (as indeed
he did), nothing would impede him from constantly advancing towards his sublime destiny—the sublime destiny open
to the poor. Just as in Chicago I had experienced the
superiority of the humble, holy life of the spirit to the worldy
life of the senses, so again in this trip through Europe I found
the contemplation of Divine truths alone complete and
satisfying.

(2)

Such contemplation was naturally evoked by the beauty of
nature: the ocean, the Lake of Geneva with its mountain

setting, the view from the Simplon pass. As my interior gaze passed from one grand truth to another, I experienced a majestic peace, a serene silence. It seemed as if my heart was completely filled with an unbounded joy. Indeed God had led me to the top of the spiritual mountain—that mountain which is Christ and His holy Catholic Church. Through its teaching and His gift of Faith, I had seen God and His creation, and the course of history from the beginning of the human race until its end, a history which contains the fall of man, his redemption, and the attainment of Heaven. From Him had poured forth into my soul great light, filling the empty canyon of my littleness. He had shown me the majestic and noble city to which I was journeying, and of which I was to become a member, a citizen of Heaven. What He thus taught me is contained in the smallest catechism of Catholic doctrine, it is revealed to all His members who open their eyes to it in Faith.

The first great truth in this scene is God Himself. God, Who is infinite happiness. He would not be God if anything were wanting to Him. He is complete and sufficient to Himself and has no need of anything else. At God's feet I saw with my mind's eye the world from the beginning to the end of time. It was very small compared to Him. No matter how long it endures, it is always finite and that is very small in comparison with the infinite. Three points in the world caught my mental eye: its beginning, its "middle" and its end. In the beginning there were two great catastrophes which were made possible by the freedom with which God had endowed angels and men. He had made them in His own image and likeness, but without His divine impeccability. Lucifer (Satan), the first of His angels, thinking to make himself like to God, had said, "I will not serve." Adam and Eve, deceived by Lucifer, had likewise fallen from innocence. Lucifer, on account of his angelic intelligence, was more guilty in the sight of God; he had foreseen more clearly the malice and consequences of his sin. He had made his choice irrevocably. Consequently he must always be separated from God. This was the beginning of Hell.

(3)

In considering Adam and Eve I remembered the condition in which they were created. As the original progenitors of the human race they had been endowed by God with certain privileges which were not due to human nature itself but were a further gift of God. These gifts were of two kinds: one group strengthened the human nature of Adam. First, as a progenitor of the human race and destined, according to God's original plan (if he were faithful) to be its teacher as well as father, Adam had been given by God complete knowledge. His body was protected from suffering, disease and death, and he was granted immunity from inordinate sensual appetites. The second gift was far greater than this first. Its object was not merely to strengthen human nature, but it was like to a second nature, which completed his humanity. This "second nature" was the state of grace, by which he had a special knowledge and love of God and in which he was made a partaker of God's own happiness. God's plan provided that the human race, after its progenitor, Adam, and its members, his children, had proved their worthiness, should see Him as He saw Himself. In disobeying God's precept, which had forbidden the use of the fruit of the tree of the knowledge of good and evil, Adam failed in the test of his worthiness. Tempted by Lucifer he was deceived into thinking he could be like to God—an independent principle of his own action. That is, his sin was a sin of pride.

(4)

It seemed to me that I could best understand my experience in the world in the light of the consequences of Adam's sin. In the world of nature, that is, in the heavens and in the plant and animal kingdom, a wonderful order reigned, but in the world of men there was disorder and confusion. Each species of plant and animal had its own design followed out by each member of that species. But of human beings, it seemed more true that each one had his own unique design, in disagreement with human nature itself. In my own personal experience, as I have mentioned, I had been aware of disordered inclinations and of great personal ignorance in respect to my end, the purpose of my existence, and the proper means to attain to it. In addition I was acutely aware of the injustice and suffering which existed in every class of mankind, and I took it for granted that man's end was death. The existence of evil had often been proposed to my mind by some of the modern philosophers as proof against the existence of Providence, or of a God. Nevertheless Adam's sin and the consequences of that sin, as recorded in the Old Testament, furnished the only explanation of evil which satisfied my intelligence. God had forewarned Adam that if he sinned he would die; the gifts given him would be taken away from him. This is precisely what happened. God took from Adam and Eve and from their children those preternatural gifts that had strengthened and guarded human nature, which would have been transmitted by Adam to his children had he been faithful. The supernatural state in which he had been established, that is, the state of grace, which was far more valuable—since through it Adam had been constituted in a state of friendship with God—was destroyed likewise by Adam's sin. God's mercy, however, which led Adam to repentance, promised him and his children a Redeemer. This Redeemer would overcome Lucifer, man's enemy, through whom man had fallen. He would come to man through a woman. Through this woman man would be restored. To Lucifer, the serpent, God had said, "I will put enmities between thee and the woman, and thy seed and her seed: she (Mary) shall crush thy head, and thou shalt lie in wait for her heel." (Gen.3:15). "For her heel": that is, for her Son, Jesus. Through Him she was to crush the head of the serpent, at the moment when the waiting serpent struck. This moment was the Crucifixion. Later I learned that Mary had also crushed the head of the serpent at the moment of her conception, through a grace, the Immaculate Conception, which the merits of the foreseen death of Jesus purchased for her. These two victories over Satan were united in this:

the one, the death of Jesus, purchased the other, the Immaculate Conception of Mary. The death of Jesus was a victory over Satan, since by it man's redemption was accomplished, by it all human sins were expiated. The Immaculate Conception was a victory over Satan because by it a human creature entered into life without the blemish of original sin, by it human nature rose from the state into which it had fallen through the artifice of the serpent.

Since the Fall of man, each individual, with the exception of the Blessed Virgin, called by Wordsworth "our tainted nature's solitary boast," has had an inclination of concupiscence, a consequence of original sin. Nevertheless, by his rational nature, man naturally tends towards God, his true end. Each makes his choice as to which of these inclinations he will follow. This explained to my mind the facts of my experience. The Catholic Faith and Catholic morality had helped me to make my choice—a choice which I felt to be not only in accord with the truth which I had learned from experience, science and philosophy, but also in harmony with my human nature. Through this choice I had attained to peace, to a greater integrity, to knowledge of myself, and to the capacity to correct my deficiencies.

This Kingdom of Truth, to which my mind turned inwardly from time to time, this vision of God and His happiness, and of the world He had created, became increasingly clear. After the creation of the angels, occurred the fall of Lucifer; later the creation of Adam and Eve in the wonderful conditions in which God had first established them; then their sin with its disastrous consequences, moral evil, death, sickness and suffering, but therewith also the promise of a Redeemer.

(5)

In the "middle" of time, the Redeemer, the promised Messiah, the Son of Mary, had come. If there was to be a complete atonement for sin, equal to the offense, it was necessary that that atonement be infinite, for an offense takes the degree of its malice from the Person against Whom it is directed. Since the Person was infinite in majesty—God Himself—the malice of the offense was infinite. Man, whose acts have only a finite value, could not make an adequate reparation. An infinite Person, however, Whose acts would have an infinite value, could. But if the reparation were to be like the offense, it must be made by a man, since man had offended. It was necessary, then, for adequate reparation, that it be made by one Person Who was both God and Man. This is what took place. Christ, Who came upon the earth in order to lay down His life in reparation to God for the injury done to God by sin, is both God and man and is but one Person, the second Person of the Blessed Trinity, called by St. John the Evangelist the "Word." Thus the human race which had begun in its first parents, Adam and Eve, had been renewed in the Second Adam, the second father of the race, Christ, Who offered His human life as a reparation for every sin of every person from the beginning to the end of time. And as to Adam Eve was given to be his helpmate in fulfilling his office as the first man, so the second man, Christ, possessed in His holy Mother Mary a helpmate in the work of redemption.

The idea of the human race descended from its divinely instituted parents, Adam and Eve, and reconstituted in its second parents Jesus and Mary, freed me from the irrational and restricting conceptions which race prejudice had fastened in my mind. In philosophy I had learned that human nature in all men is identical so that the terms "brother" and "sister" apply to us naturally. In the doctrine of the Catholic Church I found the practical realization of the unity of humankind. For all are children of Jesus and Mary, either actually or potentially. This signified, for me, that the Catholic Church is what its name implies—universal, and that its doctrine is true.

(6)

The beginning and "middle" of time were now past events. Adam and Eve had fallen, then repented and the Redeemer promised them and their children had come. The great event

in which time would end remained. That scene, called the
Final Judgment, affirmed by Christ and by His Church, was
already to my mind a clear reality. Fast upon the death of
each individual is the Particular Judgment in which is
revealed to him the consequence of the choice he has made.
Either the choice of God, to Whom one's will naturally
inclines and for Whom one has a longing God alone can
satisfy, or the choice of something other than God; that is,
one's inclination to please oneself despite the consequences,
whatsoever they may be. Since one must make a last act of
the will before one dies, there must be a last choice, after
which there can be no further choice; and this is apt to be in
accordance with the way of life he has followed. Thus, one's
place for all eternity, that is, Heaven or Hell, will be
established by one's own will and one's own choice. If it is
Heaven, one will see at once that one's part had been simply
in accepting God's grace and that one's very fidelity to grace
(including one's consent and co-operation) was God's work.
Our glory in Heaven will be the crown which God has placed
upon His own work. If one's place is Hell, one will see what
one had really known all along: that it is wholly one's own
fault and that no one else, certainly not God, is responsible.
One will see how constantly and willfully one refused the
generous and gracious offering of God's grace. Understanding God's goodness and his own malice and guilt, one will
take one's place in Hell with the full realization that only a
punishment infinite in duration can make up for the disorder
which one's guilt has caused. If there were not this place for
this person, he would, I understood, feel even more mise-
rable. The suffering, though terrible and uninterrupted,
would nevertheless not be infinite in intensity as impeni-
tence deserves, so that even in Hell God's mercy is manifested. Just as God accepts the final decision of the soul that
damns itself by its perseverance in refusing Him, so all the
Blessed in Heaven will accept the condition of the damned
(although without any satisfaction in the pain as such of the
condemned souls, which would be contrary to the charity of

the Blessed), and their everlasting happiness will not be impaired.

The Particular Judgment is the prelude to the scene of the Final Judgment at the end of the world when all the dead will rise from their graves and when the Blessed and the damned will be face to face and the lives and choices of all will be revealed to all. Then at that time will be rectified all the injustices of the present life, and the Blessed, glorified in body even as the risen Christ, will live forever their happy existence with God.—If I was to be misunderstood, it seemed to me that I could, therefore, willingly endure this for the present, for after a short while all misunderstandings would be past.

Such is the beginning, the "middle" and end of time; always present to God's view. We are living then in the Day of Christ, in the Day of Grace, in the Day of the Redeemer come, of the Promise of God fulfilled.

(7)

The first epoch of time ("the beginning") was the day of the Garden of Eden; there intervened between this time and the Incarnation (the "middle" of time) two periods: one was the period in which man was left more or less to himself with merely the promise of a Redeemer and without special external help from God to find his way. Thus, the pride of mankind had been made to see that it needed a God Who would come into its midst and make laws for it and help it even externally and socially. This God did in the next period, immediately preceding His Incarnation, when He established a special family—the Jewish race, living at first under the conditions of the agreement between God and Abraham and then under the Law which God gave to Moses. This was the time of the Circumcision, the external sign showing the incorporation of the individual into the religious body which God had established under the old dispensation. Circumcision signified the turning from sin and self-will and the acceptance of the special Law of God; it was given to the

Hebrews who were the preparation for the coming of the Messiah, the preparation for the great Church which would include all the nations. This Church was finally established by Jesus for the Jewish people and for all the nations of the earth, even until the end of time, and was the second external and social order established by God as a help for men and women in making their choice and living it, and thus finding happiness in this world, and eternal bliss in Heaven.

In this order—the order of the new dispensation, or of the New Testament—in the place of the external sign of Circumcision there is the external sign of Baptism showing the same renunciation of evil and offering of oneself to God, but, in addition, effecting inwardly that which it signifies. Until the coming of Christ man was left with the promise. The first prophecy, the Protoevangelium, had been given to Adam and Eve. Through them it had passed as a tradition to all the tribes and peoples descended from them. But in particular this promise was renewed by God in ever clearer fashion through the great Jewish prophets who foretold that this Redeemer would have two generations, a divine generation (this corresponds to the Divine Sonship of Christ) and a human generation, which would take place in Bethlehem (this was actually the birthplace of Christ). As the predicted time for His coming approached, the prophets—as the Bible testifies—became more explicit. They predicted that He would be born of a virgin and that He would die contradicted by His own people, as a leper, a man cast out, as a man of sin, through Whose stripes we would all be healed. Indeed, in the twenty-first psalm of David, the details of the Crucifixion are recounted: the piercing of Christ's hands, the offering of gall for Him to drink, the drawing of lots by the soldiers for His clothing, etc. . . .

(8)

It seems to me that by none is the Jewish race so extolled, by none presented as fulfilling so great a mission, as by the Catholic Church. The Church believes what modern Judaism questions: the entire story of the Bible; the giving of the Law by God to Moses on Mount Sinai. She believes the great Jewish prophets, whose prophecies she sees literally fulfilled. She believes the greatest of all the prophets, God Himself born of a Virgin of the Jewish race—a race which He never repudiated, not even after His death and resurrection, a race which He does not today repudiate, but rather much desires. This, it seems to me, is the true glory of the Jewish race. Or, more briefly, Jesus Christ is its glory, as the Jewish priest Simeon called Him on beholding the Infant in the Temple at Jerusalem: "A light to the revelation of the Gentiles and *the glory of thy people Israel*" (St. Luke 2:32).

From the Jewish race He chose not only His mother, but the apostles (with their great co-apostle, St. Paul) who carried His message throughout the world. Finally the first Catholic Church, the Church of Jerusalem, was entirely composed of Jews until St. Peter had a vision revealing that the Gentiles were to be admitted. At this time it was the Church's mission to make known to the entire Jewish nation that its expectation had been fulfilled, that its Messiah had come, and that all who sincerely repented of their sins were called to receive the gift of God's Holy Spirit through Baptism in the name of the Lord Jesus Christ.

(9)

On my return to New York I went to see Father Gillis again, ready for Baptism. He asked me of my plans for the future. I answered that in another month I would return to Chicago where my study of the Catholic religion had begun. Then he suggested that I wait until I returned to Chicago; there I would have an opportunity of being instructed by one of the priests in Monsignor Shannon's parish—St. Thomas the Apostle—the parish in which the University of Chicago is located. I was satisfied with that.

There I was instructed by Father Connerton. That friendly intimacy manifested by Christ during the Last Supper, I now found in His priests. By Father Connerton's meekness and charity I was prepared for Baptism more than by any other means. When he answered my questions, he did not seem to rely solely on abstract knowledge, but evidently had recourse to his personal experience of the life of grace. This impressed me anew with the practical reality of grace. Grace was in the souls of God's people, God Himself dwelt in their midst, a God with a gentleness and lowliness of which I had not before conceived.

That month was one of the happiest in my life. I felt that I was completely in the hands of God's Providence, that He would take care of and arrange all that concerned me. I had but one object: to prepare worthily for Baptism.

The desire to be baptized had in the months preceding my trip to Europe become very ardent. After I had decided to be baptized (at the time of my disclosure to Herbert that I believed) I had read Monsignor Fulton J. Sheen's book, "The Mystical Body of Christ," I saw more and more clearly that the only certain basis for human activity, the only foundation upon which man can securely build his house, is the Catholic Faith. Philosophic knowledge was not sufficient. By sin man had fallen and knowledge alone could not restore him. Sin must be atoned for, its guilt removed, the deficiencies consequent upon it corrected. For this, man needed a Redeemer, a Teacher, and the helping grace of God. In addition, philosophic knowledge of God, I now understood, could not introduce man to that intimate knowledge of God's own life which makes men and women friends of God; a knowledge which the revelation of the Lord Jesus Christ alone had brought to earth. I saw that God's plan for man was incorporation by Grace and Baptism in His Divine Son, Jesus Christ. I saw also God's wisdom in establishing, to keep intact the teaching which Jesus had brought upon earth, the authority of the Pope, the visible head of the Church, a true father of the human race, and that the reigning Holy Father is the successor in a continuous line of pontiffs from the first pontiff, St. Peter, the Rock upon which Christ had said He would build His Church. I realized also that God had ordained that the transmission of the infinite merits of His Son's satisfaction for sin be made to men through the sacraments of the Catholic Church—external signs by which grace is transmitted from God to men and women through His ministers, and that of these sacraments, Baptism is the first, and the foundation.

I came to appreciate more and more the unity of the Catholic Faith. The same Faith, the same doctrine taught by Christ and then by His apostles is taught in every Catholic parish by every Catholic priest throughout the entire world. Through this Faith, the Catholic Church presents the true knowledge of God, the Supreme Good, to all. In the Church's constitution, teaching, sacraments, and in the order of grace which it represents, I recognized those same marks of Divine authorship which as a student of natural science I had admired in the order of nature: the wonderful proportioning of means to ends, the superhuman wisdom uniting variety into a purposeful, functioning whole. I recognized this Church to be merciful and just; one, holy, Catholic and apostolic; divine; worthy of unique admiration and love; the true guide and way to the heavenly city—to God.

(10)

In my early college days, I had longed for the happiness of the entire race; now I saw that this could be achieved. Then I had thought that it could be accomplished by the application of knowledge which would ever increase in its power as it became more comprehensive and perfect. Now I saw that men and women do not have to make their own perfection, for God is their perfection: they merely need to become united to Him, by accepting Him and His Will.

Formerly social injustice had attracted me to social schemes which would replace selfishness by planned and deliberate action directed to the good of society. Thus I had been attracted to socialism, and even—since it seemed that a radical change was necessary—to communism. Yet, since I had not examined carefully those doctrines in the light of reason I did not have certitude of mind, nor the adherence of will which follows such certitude.

With my studies in philosophy in Chicago, especially with my study of logic, such certitude became for me a condition for the full acceptance of natural truth. Weighed by the standard of reason, however, the doctrines of socialism and communism were evidently wanting. Both contained in their doctrines assertions which fall under the philosophic sciences, yet contradict evident truths in these sciences, and hence are false, even absurd. With other materialists they assert that only matter is real, and they rest in those nineteenth-century errors for which twentieth-century science has ever-decreasing enthusiasm and forbearance. These errors include the belief that matter came into existence of itself or always existed, that from it, by some intrinsic power, have developed the universe, living things, plants, animals and men. This extreme evolutionary doctrine, the Marxists apply to society which likewise will evolve progressively and inevitably into a society without a political state. This social evolution will take place, according to the bolshevist communists through the medium of a bolshevistic revolutionary dictatorship, which will continue its terrorism and bloodshed until all its subjects have acquired the communistic mentality and are fit members of an anarchistic society.

It was during my studies in Chicago that the error of the theory of extreme evolutionism became apparent to me. The application of this theory to society involved, I now realized, many other absurdities. Thus its principle of determinism was contrary to the freedom of the wills of human beings. I now knew that the human will is, after the Providence of God (which is able to direct to its own ends even the perverse acts of His creatures' wills), the real power determining the course of human history. But the will is free—that is, a man can change his views, his course of action, etc. The *inevitable* evolution of a communistic society is an absurdity, for society consists of individuals whose wills are free. Communism denies not only the freedom of the will, but also all rights: individual, family or state, as well as the natural moral law. Falsehood, theft and murder are justified if they are directed to its ends. Hence, I realized, no one living under such a regime can have any security, not even its progenitors and rulers. The Russian communists' extermination of each other confirms this conclusion. What appealed to me in communism I found now to be primitive Christian principle and practice, e.g., esteem for the poor and distribution to each according to need, which the first Church of Jerusalem had introduced. Despite the communist's denial of morality, I could see that external justice was what he sought. But I saw that his ideal was confused by a concept intrinsically impossible, and hence impossible of realization, namely anarchism: a society without a state. Finally, communism required an absolute faith in its leaders: men who deny all morality yet in whose hands we are asked to place all power.

Anarchism indeed I saw was an impossibility. Reason makes evident that the true origin of society is not in a social contract, or from chance, but is founded in man's nature itself, which is social. The true origin of society consequently is in God, the Author of human nature. Authority, whether it reposes in all the members of the state, as in a democracy, or in representatives chosen by them as in a republic, in a few as in an aristocracy or in one as in a monarchy, is a necessary element of society. Civil authority is a necessary servant of the common good, the end of society; a just authority protects the rights of the citizens, and establishes conditions conducive to the development of their powers of mind, and heart, and body. This it does, for example, by regulating the instruments of social good by just laws providing for the public health, education, public order, decency, etc. The citizens of a society without a political state would, even if they were angels, be bereft of that direction in the pursuit of common undertakings which authority provides. But anarchism is a society without a state, without government, without authority.

Besides their denial of the truth of reason, communism and socialism, I now for the first time realized, are entirely ignorant of the content of the Revelation which God has made known to men. Thus they know nothing of the fulfillment of the Jewish religion and Jewish prophecies which, as I had discovered, is found in Christ and His Church. They are ignorant of the supernatural character of the Church, of its sacraments and the life of grace to which they minister. They do not recognize that the external disorder which they seek to correct has its origin in the internal disorder of sin which must likewise be corrected.

The Church's teaching, on the other hand, I was now certain, provides the proper order for human desire, according to the teaching of Christ, "Seek first the kingdom of God and his justice and all these things shall be given to you besides" (Matt. 6:33). Subject to this primary end, it proposes the true principles of social justice by which all present day evils can be corrected and hence it fosters material and social progress and that full development of the individual's natural powers which civil society is charged with promoting and protecting.

The happiness of the human race, then, was not to be achieved by the perfection of the external order alone, but primarily by the correction of the internal disorder of sin, through union with God. But union with God, I had found, required the acceptance of the Redeemer, Teacher and Giver of grace, Jesus Christ, through faith in His divinity and in His doctrine, and through Baptism which remits sin and incorporates the faithful as members of His Mystical Body into Jesus Christ, true God and true man, the Head. Through His merits alone is man justified.

After my Baptism, which took place on November 6, 1936, all that had been promised was fulfilled. I knew myself to be truly reborn, and possessed of a new life. This was also very evident to my friends, as their remarks showed. By Baptism, by the coming into my soul of the Father, Son and Holy Spirit in sanctifying grace, I had been truly given a new life which completely satisfied every desire of my heart. My mind was at rest, my intelligence and reason completely satisfied in the wonderful agreement of the Catholic Faith with reason and experience. My heart was likewise completely satisfied. I had attained the end for which I was created. I knew my Creator,

I loved Him and I was going to enjoy His happiness forever. I now had, not only reason and the determination which proceeds from reason, to help me overcome interior and exterior difficulties, but also divine grace, which God, in His wonderful goodness, poured forth in abundance. He kept my heart at peace in every circumstance. I had but one desire: to follow Christ, Who had come into the world to do His Father's Will—to place my life entirely at His disposal.

CHAPTER FIVE

FULFILLMENT: GOD DWELLS WITH
THE SPIRITUAL DESCENDANTS
OF THE JEWS

(1) In the Catholic Church I find God, dwelling in the midst of His people, the spiritual descendants of the Jews.

(2) God's signature is on this Church: the miracles He works in it.

(3) The Church is holy: Her activity on behalf of men.

(4) My life in the Church: all my desires are fulfilled.

(5) In the Church: my external life: psychiatry, family, friends.

(6) In the Church: culmination in the religious life: the perfect Christian life. Reality of Jesus Christ. Perfect union with Jesus, the ideal of the religious life, is not a delusion: proof from the visible achievements of contemplatives.

(7) Source of true life is the life of prayer. Mary the Mother of Jesus and our Mother: a source of the knowledge of Jesus, and the Cross of Christ. The holy rosary and its Mysteries.

(8) The Holy Spirit and His preaching of the Word of God is the Source of true and everlasting life and of the life of prayer. His preaching to and about the Jews through St. Peter and St. Paul. "The gifts and the call of God (to the Jews, to be His people) are without repentance."

(9) The glorification of the Blessed Virgin Mary, Mother of God, Mother of fair love, Mother of grace. Her charming motherly lowliness.

(10) Holy Mary's "Magnificat," and mine, and yours if you will: "He has given help to Israel, his servant, mindful of His mercy—even as He spoke to our fathers—to Abraham and to his posterity forever."

(1)

Thus did I, a Jew, without becoming less a Jew, become a Catholic. Since then the expectation of my Baptism has been fulfilled; the life into which I was born has continued, ever growing greater; this life is the life of God.

In my childhood I had had the impression that the ancient Jews had God in their midst; in the Catholic Church I found the spiritual descendants of these Jews and that God was still in their midst. In a most sacred prayer of Holy Mass, when the Precious Blood of Jesus Christ is offered for the redemption of all from the slavery of sin, the Church prays that its sacrifice may be acceptable as was the "the sacrifice of Abraham, our Patriarch." These words of the Mass were referred to by the late Pope Pius XI. When discussing the question whether Catholics could be anti-Semites, he said, "Spiritually *we are* Semites." Christ is in the midst of His children, the seed of Abraham, to whom He said when He was about to die: "I will not leave you orphans." He is still really present amongst them (although also at the right hand of the Father), through His Presence in the Blessed Sacrament in the Tabernacles of His Church. He is also present in the hearts of all in the state of grace, and is in His priests, who are the humble servants of His people, and of all mankind. In that conversation of the heart in which audible words are not used, that is, in mental prayer, He, the Good Shepherd with wonderful love and friendship guides and counsels His sheep, leading them to pasture. Yet, lest there be any self-deception, He has given to humans the priest who, in confession and spiritual guidance, is an external and objective confirmation of the way in which Christ leads the soul inwardly; for Christ speaks through the priest who is united to his bishop and the Pope, i.e. to the Church's teaching authority, having said, "Who hears you, hears Me." The Catholic Faith and Catholic morality are objectively true. The priest who has studied its truths (which are safeguarded by the Church's teaching and sound theology), and in whom Christ through His Holy Spirit dwells, is able to render service to the faithful individually, helping them to avoid the pitfalls and deceptions to which human nature is prone.

(2)

My experience as a Catholic, like that of other practicing Catholics, leaves no doubt about the reality of the supernatural character of the Church, and of God's presence and operation in it and in its members. His signature—which no one can forge—is miracles. A miracle is a true sign, visible in the world, of God. Miracles have been the mark of the true Church of God since the resurrection of Christ, as before Christ they were the mark of the authenticity of the Jewish religion.

Two world famous examples of recent times may be mentioned. One is Lourdes, where the Blessed Virgin Mary appeared in 1858 to Bernadette Soubirous, asking that a shrine be built. Here many miracles of healing have occurred. For many decades a medical bureau of Catholic and non-Catholic doctors has authenticated a number of these cures as occurring in a manner which is naturally inexplicable.

Another is Fatima, Portugal. Here an outstanding event in the history of miracles took place in 1917 when the Blessed Virgin Mary appeared, predicting the second world war and telling the conditions under which her divine Son would grant peace. At that time she told the children to whom she was confiding her mission (and who were accompanied by an ever increasing crowd of people in her five successive appearances), that there would be a striking miracle so that all might believe, and this miracle, witnessed by 70,000 people, was recorded by the secular newspapers of the time.[1]

---

[1] See "Note on the Solar Prodigy of Fatima."

(3)

Another sign of the Presence of God in the midst of men is the sanctity of the Church and her activity on behalf of men. The Catholic Church proposes an ideal of sanctity for all. This has a practical expression in the evangelical chastity of the priesthood, in the religious Orders of the Church and in the dedication to the Gospel values of many of the laity. The Church has been the unique custodian of the wisdom of the past (the philosophical and theological tradition), of civil rights (which were developed in Catholic England and Catholic Europe), and it is the unique defender of human nature against the attacks, on the one hand, of communism, socialism, nazism and fascism which seek to deprive the individual of his rights and to enslave him to the state, and against false doctrines, on the other hand, such as Freudianism, materialism, extreme evolutionism and other errors which would deny man the power of reason and freedom of the will. In the spiritual ascendancy of the Papacy at the present time many non-Catholics see the hope of the modern world and, in the proposals which it has made since the nineteenth century through Pope Leo XIII and his successors, non-Catholics and Catholics see the promise of the new social order in which the evils of capitalism and industrialism will be overcome by a new system of profit sharing in which the workers and industrialists will be united.

In the "restoration of all things in Christ" lies the promise of a renewal of the arts, music, literature, architecture and philosophy, while science itself will profit by a revival of philosophy and the spread of the Catholic Faith.

The vitality of the Catholic Church is shown in the conversions which are taking place in all parts of the world. An example is that of Africa where half a million are converted yearly. Another is the conversion of the intellectuals, who, since the Oxford movement, especially, and the conversion of John Henry Newman, have been entering the Church in a steady stream.

(4)

The sudden change and interruption in the course of the relations of God with His Chosen People, which impressed me in my early youth, I now saw had taken place at the time of the death of Christ. Previous to that time God did dwell in the midst of the Jewish people. Subsequent to that time, the mission of the Jews to bring forth the Redeemer having been fulfilled, and the Catholic Church, the Church of all the nations, having been established, God has dwelt in the midst of it. Here He shall remain until the time of the Last Judgment as He has said.

In the second period of my life, in the time of my high school and college education, I had felt an intense longing for personal perfection and the perfection and happiness of the human race. I had felt a desire for "all." This is a natural longing of the soul—it belongs to human nature. Each of us has an infinite desire. We are not free to determine our end. We can place it mistakenly in creatures, in honors, fame, wealth, bodily necessities, health, pleasure, knowledge, virtue—but each of these is but a means to an end, each is finite and therefore our infinite desire cannot be satisfied by any one of these. This explains the restless and insatiable search for "more and more." Thus those who try to make creatures their end, find no rest. Only in God can the will rest. Likewise our will basically desires the unity and happiness of all, and this merely because in our essential nature we are identical. That is, we each have the same specific nature, and our will desires the infinite happiness of all. I found now, in my practical life, what I had previously understood in the days of study at the University of Chicago and in the time of my instructions before entering the Church: in grace, these natural longings are fulfilled. Grace perfects and completes our nature. It remits sin which blocks the will and blinds the mind and prevents our knowing and loving God and our fellow creatures as we ought; through grace, we obtain our natural and supernatural happiness. The Heart of Jesus Christ, as His life and death show, was set on offering Himself as a sacrifice to His Father for the sins of all His people, the human race, that God might be all in all. Such, it seems to me, ought also to be the heart of every perfect disciple, of every perfect Christian. Through the conversion of society to the Church and to its God will come about that social perfection for which I had hoped in my early youth, a social perfection far richer than I then dreamed—springing from a common and eternal possession of the boundless riches of God.

I experienced the love of the Sacred Heart and His generosity when He first introduced me to His life by the actual grace of Faith which led to my Baptism. Upon being baptized I had the feeling of a great achievement, a final and ultimate achievement; I had reached my goal and I was completely satisfied. At the same time this experience was made the richer by the realization that there was absolutely no merit on my part, that this achievement was an outright gift of God, to which I had no claim. Now by Baptism the guilt of every thought, word, deed or omission of my entire life was remitted, forgiven by God, and with them all the punishment due to them. I hated sin as the only great evil, and I loved God and His Commandments. This was the work of God enlightening me to know good and evil during the months preceding my Baptism, and drawing me to the love of good and hatred of evil. This is "conversion." I came to know how imbedded I had been in ignorance, error, prejudice and vice—in a word, in sin and its effects. I felt moved to believe myself the least of men and the farthest removed from God. This enabled me to appreciate the depth of His mercy and goodness and it gave me the conviction that no one need be without hope. In fact, the only object for which God can possibly act is His own honor; any other object would be unworthy of Him; and God cannot act unworthily. The more embittered a soul is against Him the further it is from Him and the more in need it is of His compassion. Mercy is drawn by need. His goodness and mercy are shown forth and His honor achieved in coming to the aid of such a soul. I felt this to be true in my case, and experienced a great sympathy with others who remained in the predicament in which I had been.

My heart was completely satisfied in the attainment of my end, God. I saw opening up before me the possibility of unlimited growth in His knowledge, love and service. Each day would be an opportunity, by fidelity to his grace, to merit to be closer to Him for all eternity.

In the time of my friendship with Herbert Schwartz and Herbert Ratner I had come to appreciate the richness of friendship and the value of a sincere heart. Now I found all that is good in friendship verified in my friendship with Christ. In prayer I found in Him a wonderful sympathy and understanding, while by His grace He purified and strengthened my intention and will. I knew that He alone could fully understand me and His help was not wanting in satisfying the desires of my heart. On the other hand, as He revealed to me His own Heart (as He did, first of all in the Scriptures), I learned more and more how to understand Him and make His interests my own. I regret that I have been a very dull pupil, but I rejoice that He has put up with me. Since my entrance into the Catholic Church the wonderful life of prayer, which is the intimate relation of the human heart to God in friendship and love, became the first expression of my new life. This prayer was supported by study of the Catholic religion, and found expression in fidelity to my daily duties and an increasing sympathy and love of people.

Before my entrance into the Catholic Church, I had grown stronger in my motive of seeking first the kingdom of God and His Justice. This meant to me to seek absolutely and first the truth and to make my life entirely consistent with first truth. This meant also to be devout, to be given to God, and such became my determination. God has made our trust in His Providence and the giving of ourselves a condition for His best care, and I found that He did not fail those who trust in Him. Quickly following this determination came the grace of Faith and my entrance into the Church, and since then He has arranged all things for my best interest.

One last obstacle to a love of the Church was removed in a time preceding my Baptism through the reading of a letter sent by the federation of Rabbis of France to the Holy Father. It testified the gratitude of the Jewish people to the Church for its friendship for the Jews, and recorded the history of Papal protection during times of persecution. I had not known, for example, that at the time of the Spanish Inquisition, the Papal lands were open to persecuted Jews as a place of refuge and that there they had received kind treatment. All bitterness against the Church now left my heart, bitterness laid up perhaps in school days and whose presence I had not realized until then.

(5)

At this time, when I had found true happiness and basic truth, which all seek, my outward life underwent an unexpected change. Professor McKeon decided that the report I had prepared for the Josiah Macy, Jr. Foundation was unsatisfactory and unworthy of presentation for a continuation of the grant under which I had been working with him.

My spiritual director, Father Timothy Sparks, O.P., told me that the Oak Park Hospital would consider accepting me as an interne. On January 1, 1937, two months after my Baptism, I began an interneship there. This hospital is conducted by the Soeurs de Misericorde, to whom I am indebted for many kindnesses.

Eager to make some return to my parents for their love and affection, and to fulfill the desire of my mother who asked me to return East, I made application for a psychiatric interneship in New York City. Through the recommendation of a friend whom I had recently made, Dr. Jascha Kasanin, a Jewish psychoanalyst, I obtained an interneship in the psychiatric division of Bellevue Hospital, which began July 1, 1937. After completing this interneship I received an appointment in the New York State Psychiatric Service at the Brooklyn State Hospital. After nine months, I was invited

by a Catholic institution, Lincoln Hall (the successor to the
Catholic Protectory), which was just opening, to institute a
psychiatric department. During the time of my medical and
psychiatric service I was always intimate with my colleagues,
whether Jewish or Gentile, while my capacity for work and
obedience had increased. Work and obedience were a great
joy for I was working for God.

I had been away from home, except for vacations, since I
had begun my college education in 1925 until nine months
after my Baptism when, on July 1, 1937, I began my
interneship at Bellevue. Now I spent many evenings and
week-ends with my parents. With my father I had the great
happiness of an ever-deepening fellowship, and this extended even into matters Catholic, for he would attend the
lectures of the Catholic Thought Association given by the
Dominican Fathers, together with me, and was fond of the
priests, in particular of Father Walter Farrell, O.P., with
whom he had a few long conversations. Mother accompanied
me occasionally to Catholic religious services; she was
impressed to find in them much that reminded her of Jewish
religious customs, and she was struck by the devotion of the
people. I also associated with my other relations from time to
time, finding a deeper affection for them since I had become
a Catholic, while with them and others I was frank about
being a Jew by race and a Catholic by religion. Similarly I had
many associations among Catholics, both in the priesthood,
in the religious state and among the laity, Miss Marie
Murtaugh—now dead—and Mr. Charles Rich, a convert from
Judaism especially. I was a member of a small guild, the
Sedes Sapientiae, which was instituted in honor of the
Blessed Virgin Mary, the Seat of Wisdom, by Miss Dominica
Kaluznic, and was presided over by a Franciscan Father,
Father Oliver Murray. Its object was the growth of its
members in the interior life, especially through true devotion
to the Mother of God (taught with special clarity by Saint
Louis-Marie Grignion De Montfort), through daily mental
prayer and attendance of Holy Mass and reception of Holy

Communion, weekly confessions and recourse to a spiritual director.

A few months after my entrance into the Church, Herbert Schwartz, to whom I am so deeply indebted for the grace of being a Catholic, was himself baptized together with his wife, and about a year later Herbert Ratner took the same step after considerable study; three of the Jewish girls who had been numbered among our intimate friends became Catholics, one, after four years, entering a religious society, the Grail. We, together with a few other Catholics at the University, formed a chapter of the Third Order of St. Dominic attached to the Dominican House of Studies at River Forest, Illinois. I chose one of the Dominican Fathers of this House (Father Timothy M. Sparks) as my spiritual director after entering the Church, and his counsel and prayers proved invaluable.

With priests and religious I always felt as much at home as with any member of my family, and it seemed just as natural for them to call me by my first name or even by my nickname, "Bud." In confession and spiritual direction, contrary to what one might naturally expect, I found that they always stimulated a spirit of initiative rather than of dependence. "Of initiative," that is, of docility to the Holy Spirit, Who is given individually and personally to each of the faithful.

(6)

In November 1940, at a time when opportunities for psychiatric advancement were opening to me, God indicated that He had other designs and made me realize that the time had come to enter religious life,[2] to which I had, from the time of my Baptism, been attracted. I had been given an everlasting happiness and knew that one thing only remained unsettled in the world. God is complete and is complete

---

[2] The religious life is a state freely embraced by those who consecrate themselves to God by professing out of love of Him the gospel counsels of poverty, chastity, and obedience according to a Rule, in a community.

happiness. For the dead, the issue is settled. Those who have died in the state of friendship with God are in complete happiness in Heaven, or, after their final purgation (Purgatory), will be admitted to Heaven. But in the world many souls live in a state in which the issue has not been settled. The real battle-front is against sin and the real spoils to be won are souls who will be our companions in everlasting happiness.

For these spoils, the religious enlists in the militia of Jesus Christ. He fights for the love of God and of His Divine Son. Yet his life is not only a warfare but a Paradise regained, for he enjoys the full fruits of the Incarnation and Redemption, especially in his life of prayer, in which he participates ever more fully in the life of God, with Whom, if he is faithful, he will dwell for all eternity.

The religious, by his profession or vows, not only makes profession of Faith in the Divinity of Jesus Christ and puts himself entirely at the Lord's disposal, but also does so in the manner which conforms to the invitation which Jesus Himself issued: "If you will be perfect, leave all that you possess and follow Me."

All, through adoption of the Catholic Faith, are called to a life of sanctity. Indeed, sanctity is the only reasonable ideal of life. Sanctity for the Catholic is to be found in increasing union with Jesus Christ, and in the perfect fulfillment of the duties of one's state of life. But the religious state, and especially the monastic state, makes union with Jesus Christ into a state of life. The monk or nun has but a single end in view, to which his or her entire life is exclusively directed. This end is the very end of man, God. Union with Christ means participation in the sentiments and dispositions of the Word made flesh. Christ, the Archetype of men and women is God's ideal for them, given them as the mode of their sanctification. This sanctification itself provides a remedy for human weakness, since it effects the integration and development of human nature and its faculties. *Indeed, my book,* Hammer and Fire, *published in 1958, deals with this subject.* Human methods, such as self-improvement, psy-

choanalysis, perfection of the individual through membership in a perfect state, etc., have not achieved this goal, and
cannot. While God's remedy does not remove sufferings, it
shows how they can become a means to happiness, as means
for the satisfaction of one's own sins and those of others,
after the example of Jesus. God's grace strengthens, supports, and rejoices those who suffer in this spirit, so as often
to render the moments of suffering the happiest moments of
life.

These truths I have experienced for myself. If Jesus Christ
were not God, were not reigning at the right hand of the
Father, religious would be the victims of a delusion, and their
entire life, built as it is on this truth, would be madness. Yet,
on the contrary, religious especially are provided with the
means for achieving that perfection of character and life
which all men recognize as most noble: a life sincerely
devoted to the welfare of others and to the suppression of
selfish self-interest, in the midst of hardship and suffering.
Likewise those traits which modern people, for example
psychiatrists, agree are unsound, are the very traits which
religious morality (the perfect expression of Catholic morality) rejects; for the religious life fosters a cheerful, simple
acceptance of contradiction, and of opposition; an inner
readiness to fulfill the will of legitimate authority; a devotion
to duty and to the welfare of others at one's own expense;
the suppression of complaining, excusing, restless dissatis-
faction, and of peculiarities and eccentricities of judgment
and temperament.

To achieve this the religious (and the Christian) must ever
repudiate anew his or her own peculiar weaknesses. The
example of perfection which he or she has before his eyes is
that of his Leader, the meek, humble, obedient, patient,
loving Jesus, his Lord. The strength by which he achieves
success is the grace of Jesus Christ, by which these virtues
are infused into his soul. Failures to correspond with this
Ideal, to act in accordance with the gift of God's grace,
furnish matter for fresh acts of humility, meekness, submission and patience. That the one who fails to resemble this

Ideal can humbly avow it and thus be united to Him, is a solace for me. The examples of religious life are supplied by many saints who fulfilled its aim. In their marvelous achievements is offered a fresh proof of the reality and efficacy of God's plan for man's restoration and happiness. Saint Francesca Xavier Cabrini, the first canonized citizen-Saint of the United States, is a good example. For love of the Sacred Heart of Jesus and in union with His dispositions, drawing her strength from an intense and continual life of prayer, she founded sixty-six convents, schools, orphanages and hospitals in the United States, South America and Europe. Despite frail health, in the midst of sickness she pursued her work, full of joy and cheerfulness, and with an ever-ready obedience, by which she submitted her will and judgment to that of the authority which represented the will of the God she served. *Mother Teresa of Calcutta is another example.*

The Cistercian Order of the Strict Observance, the Order of St. Benedict and of St. Bernard, has likewise furnished examples of the fruitfulness of the life of prayer in the union with Jesus Christ as manifested by visible human achievements. In the course of its history, illustrious members have been taken out of its ranks by the Church—especially in the Middle Ages—and have manifested in their services for men and women, the fruits of the religious character which is formed in the cloister after the counsel and pattern of its Lord.

Such has been my external life since my entrance into the Church, with its culmination in the religious state.

(7)

My real life, since the day of my baptism, has been a life of prayer. In this life I have discovered in the Mother of Christ my true mother. Since Christ is one single Individual, both God and man in one Person, the Second Person of the Blessed Trinity, His mother is truly the Mother of God. For a mother gives birth not to a nature, but to a person, and in Christ, although there are two natures—both distinct and perfect—there is but one Person. Man by grace is reborn into a real participation in the life of Christ, truly present in his soul. Christ is the Head, the faithful are His members, together they form one mystical body. And together they have one mother. And as the expectant mother is mother of her unborn child, so is the Mother of Jesus mother of the non-Catholic, who as yet is unborn into the life of the Church. Mary is the spiritual mother of all.

That she is my mother, I have experienced. Through her eyes I came to know Jesus and His sacrifice better. As I made the Stations of the Cross, the real significance of the crucifixion became more evident. I saw that His crucified arms were really outstretched to embrace each as His brother and sister, and to include each in His love. Jesus made no exceptions. His sacrifice on the cross was offered by Him as atonement for every sin of every one from the beginning to the end of the world. Having a perfect human heart He had a love for His countrymen the Jews, which has never changed, and His arms are especially held out towards them. Thus His Church has a special Congregation, Notre Dame de Sion, which was founded to offer continual prayer and sacrifice to God for the welfare, happiness and conversion of the Jewish people.

The Cross came to mean to me the sign of the contradiction of God by man since man contradicted God's providential plan for his happiness. But it came to mean much more than this, since God, Who in His wisdom entered the world in the form of a man and subjected Himself to the divine laws for creatures, changed the tragedy into a blessing. He made the Cross the symbol of God's love for all, and through it His Church invites all to profit by His sacrifice. I know myself to be as truly the cause of the death of Jesus as any other member of the human race since He died to atone for my sins as well as for the sins of others. To God, the past, present and future are all present and Jesus, foreseeing how each individual would use his free will, obtained for each the opportunity of forgiveness.

It was, however, especially in the mysteries of the holy rosary that through Our Lady's eyes I came to know of the life of Jesus. The five joyful mysteries propose to the mind the first thirty years of the life of Jesus on earth, as related in the Gospels. His life began with His conception at the time of the Annunciation. The angel Gabriel asked the Blessed Virgin's consent to the divine purpose, explaining that God destined her to be the mother of the Messiah. (The opening words of the Hail Mary—the prayer that rises to heaven daily from millions of hearts and has done so for centuries—recall the dialogue between Mary and the angel Gabriel). The second joyful mystery recalls the sanctification of St. John the Baptist in the womb of his mother Elizabeth on the occasion of the visit of her cousin, the Blessed Virgin Mary, through the efficacy of Her unborn Jesus. The third joyful mystery commemorates the birth of Jesus Christ in Bethlehem; the fourth His Presentation; the fifth His converse with the Rabbis of the Temple at the age of twelve, where His mother and St. Joseph found Him after a three days' search.

During the first thirty years of His life, Jesus was obedient to His mother and to His foster father, St. Joseph. They lived the life of a Jewish family.

Then follow the five sorrowful mysteries whose object is His suffering and death. His death was not the only sorrow which the Blessed Mother endured during this time. He had foreseen the destruction of Jerusalem, soon to occur. Gazing at the holy city and weeping in pity for the fate awaiting his countrymen, He had said: "If thou hadst known, in this thy day, even thou, the things that are for thy peace!" (Luke 19:42). His sentiments were echoed by those of His sorrowful Mother. They are expressed by the lamentations of Jeremiah written by that prophet in regard to the destruction of Jerusalem at the time of the Babylonian captivity, but expressive of the grief of Jesus, Mary and of their Church over the final ruin of the Jewish Nation, following soon after His death. These lamentations are sung in grave tones of Hebrew melody, on the three days preceding Good Friday in the Tenebrae service of the Church. The ruin of Jerusalem under the Roman general Titus in 70 A.D. was symbolic of the ruin of the many Jewish people who, following their leaders, abandoned the true religion of God. Lovingly, in its beautiful Tenebrae Service, the Church appeals for the return of the Jews: "Jerusalem, Jerusalem turn thee to the Lord, thy God." The sorrow of the Blessed Mother over the fall of her Hebrew children, which crushed her most pure heart, is further expressed in these words, "Great as the sea is thy destruction." Of herself and her divine Son, she says, through the voice of Holy Church: "O all you who pass by the way, attend and see, if there be sorrow like unto my sorrow" (Jeremiah 1:12). The way she alludes to is the way of the Cross, the way trodden by Jesus. By this way all pass. Some blindly, not seeing the Savior close by, bearing His redeeming Cross. Others indifferently. Others stop to mock and deride Him. Still others stop to consider His beauty—and catching His loving glance, follow Him to Cavalry—and to the glory of His resurrection.

It was not until the time of His death that Jesus Christ instituted the priesthood of the Catholic Church. He had faithfully fulfilled the Mosaic Law, even during the course of the Last Supper. At that time, one of His disciples, Judas, had gone forth to the High Priest, who had agreed upon His death. His rejection by the Head of the Jewish Priesthood (who was also the Head of the Sanhedrin) being consummated, Jesus instituted the Catholic hierarchy in the persons of the Apostles (Luke 22:22). After this He went forth to the place to which Judas was bringing the party who were to capture Him. The sorrowful mysteries proceed to the scourging of Jesus by the Roman soldiers, and to the crowning of thorns. This mockery of His kingship of the Jews, He bore with dignity and meekness, knowing that through His example men would be enabled to endure in union with Him the indignities which would befall them. Then is commemorated the carrying of the holy Cross, symbolic of human life, which for all men has its sufferings and humiliations. These are easier to endure with meekness and humility when men keep before their eyes the example of their God and Savior.

Finally in the mystery of the crucifixion is unfurled the standard of victory. All who fight under this banner obtain the trophy of everlasting life.

(8)

In the glorious mysteries of the rosary, the Resurrection is commemorated first. It was during the time of His Resurrection that Christ confirmed Peter's commission as the head of His Church and as the first Pontiff (John 21:15–17; see Matt. 16:17–19). During this time He gave the Apostles their mission to go forth and teach all nations, baptizing them in the name of the Blessed Trinity. Then while they looked on, He ascended heavenward until a cloud concealed Him from their view. By this wonderful event, He manifested that the place to which, by a locomotion peculiar to the resurrected, He was ascending, was a real place, a place which would be the location of His glorious body—that Heaven is a reality. He also thus made known the property of agility belonging to the resurrected body, whose motion is not dependent on the law of gravity, but corresponds to the personal will, as freely as do one's thoughts. Thus, after the general resurrection, the blessed, who see and perfectly love God, have a bodily life conformable to such an exalted state. After this mystery, the promised advent of the Holy Spirit is commemorated as the third of the glorious mysteries. As the instrument of the Holy Spirit, Peter immediately preached the first sermon to the Jews, at which time three thousand were converted as is related in Acts 2:22–47:

"Men of Israel, hear these words. Jesus of Nazareth was a man approved by God among you by miracles and wonders and signs, which God did through him in the midst of you, as you yourselves know. Him, when delivered up by the settled purpose and foreknowledge of God, you have crucified and slain by the hands of wicked men. But God has raised him up, having loosed the sorrows of hell, because it was not possible that he should be held fast by it. . . . This Jesus God has raised up, and we are all witnesses of it. Therefore, exalted by the right hand of God, and receiving from the Father the promise of the Holy Spirit, he has poured forth this spirit which you see and hear. For David did not ascend into heaven, but he says himself,

'The Lord said to my Lord:
Sit thou at my right hand,
until I make thy enemies
a footstool for thy feet.'
"Therefore, let all the house of Israel know most assuredly that God has made both Lord and Christ, this Jesus whom you crucified."
Now on hearing this they were pierced to the heart and said to Peter and the rest of the apostles, "Brethren, what shall we do?"
But Peter said to them, "Repent and be baptized every one of you in the name of Jesus Christ for the forgiveness of your sins; and you will receive the gift of the Holy Spirit. For to you is the promise and to your children and to all who are far off, even to all whom the Lord our God calls."

While the Jews were the first fruits of the sacrifice of Jesus, the Gentiles became the fullness of His fruit and of His Church. As St. Paul, the great apostle of the Gentiles, says, in the Holy Scriptures (Romans 10:12):

. . . there is no distinction between Jew and Greek, for there is the same Lord of all, rich towards all who call upon him. "For whoever calls upon the name of the Lord shall be saved."

At that time the Jewish synagogues persecuted the first Christians, but the Christians, on the contrary, were forbidden to shut the Church against the Jews. St. Paul likened the Jews to natural branches of an olive tree into which wild branches—the Gentiles—had been grafted. If wild branches could be engrafted, he says, how much more so the natural branches. The Church is always open to Jews.

I say then: Has God cast off his people By no means! For I also am an Israelite by the posterity of Abraham, of the tribe of Benjamin. God has not cast off his people whom he foreknew. . . .
I say then: have they so stumbled as to fall? By no means! But by their offense salvation has come to the Gentiles, that they may be jealous of them. Now if their offense is the riches of the world, and their decline the riches of the Gentiles, how much more their full number!
. . . For if the rejection of them is the reconciliation of the world, what will the reception of them be but life from the dead? Now if the first handful of the dough is holy, so also is the lump of dough; and if the root is holy, so also are the branches. But if some of the branches have been broken off, and if thou, being a wild olive, are grafted in their place, and hast become a partaker of the stem and fatness of the olive tree, do not

boast against the branches. But if thou dost boast, still it is not thou that supportest the stem, but the stem thee. . . .

And they also, if they do not continue in unbelief, will be grafted in; for God is able to graft them back. For if thou hast been cut off from the wild olive tree which is natural to thee, and contrary to nature, hast been grafted into the cultivated olive tree, how much more shall these, the natural branches, be grafted into their own olive tree!

. . . For the gifts and the call of God are without repentance.

For as you also at one time did not believe God, but now have obtained mercy by reason of their unbelief, so they too have not now believed by reason of the mercy shown you, that they too may obtain mercy. For God has shut up all in unbelief, that he may have mercy upon all.

Oh, the depth of the riches of the wisdom and of the knowledge of God! How incomprehensible are his judgments and how unsearchable his ways! For

"Who has known the mind of the Lord,
   or who has been his counsellor?
Or who has first given to him,
   that recompense should be made him?"
For from him and through him and unto him are all things.
To him be the glory forever, amen.

(Romans 11:1–36)

Thus the third glorious mystery of the holy rosary introduces us to the preaching of the Church by Jews to Jews and foreshadows the preaching to the Gentiles. In St. Peter's discourse, the promise of the gift of the Holy Spirit is made to the Jews, to their children, "and to all who are far off"—even to the present generation. From St. Paul's discourse it appears that the Jews, who stumbled at the time of Christ's death, have not fallen; that rejected, they are eventually to be received in full number. "For the gifts and the call of God are without repentance." Finally that this return of the Jews to the Faith of their fathers, to the God of the patriarchs and prophets, will cause a renewal of holy Church. The rejection of the Jews led to the entrance into the Church of the nations of the world. The reception into the Church of the full number of the Jews will surely recall the nations which have fallen from her Faith and unity, "life from the dead," as well as those who have never known her. Thus in the unity of one Faith, one charity and in one name can be wrought society's unity and perfection.

(9)

The fourth and fifth mysteries reveal the reward which God had in store for His Blessed Mother and are the only ones not narrated in the gospels. After her death Mary was assumed into Heaven. It was fitting that as Christ rose from the dead, His body and soul reunited in perfect human nature, so also the Mother who had given him that body should be reunited in body and soul in anticipation of the general resurrection from the dead; and be thus taken into Heaven, and there crowned sovereign of angels and men. The Blessed Virgin Mary was, even at the moment of her conception, given by God a unique position in the human race. In view of the foreseen merits of the Passion of Jesus, and in order to prepare for Him and us a worthy mother, she alone of all mankind was excepted from the stain of original sin. She was conceived in a state of superabounding grace, contrary to the lot of the rest of men upon whom the sin of Adam and its consequences justly fall. The native condition of the Blessed Virgin becomes our condition too, though in far lesser degree, and in a different manner, by the saving waters of baptism. It was fitting that the Mother of Jesus Christ should be conceived immaculate. It was fitting that, having served her God and men and women faithfully in poverty and humiliations throughout her life, she should be crowned Queen of Heaven and earth after her death.

Yet as this great Queen remains now as humble and maternal as when she cared for the Infant Jesus. This she has shown in the circumstances of her appearances on earth. Thus, when she had a message for the Universal Church and the human race in 1858, she appeared to the little Bernadette, whom she made to feel perfectly at home in her company. Again, at Fatima, near Lisbon, in Portugal, on May 13, 1917, and during the five following months, she appeared to shepherd children and manifested anew her love.[3] When she appeared in America—in Mexico (an event now commemorated by the feast of Our Lady of Guadalupe), it was to

---

[3] See "Note on the Solar Prodigy of Fatima."

a lowly Aztec Indian, Juan Diego, to whom she entrusted her mission. Through these appearances, her wonderful lowliness, her maternal fondness and her charm and loveliness have won the hearts of many. Mary, the mother of men, is "more a mother than a queen." Anyone who has difficulties in the path of becoming a Catholic or in advancing in perfection may experience for himself her kindness by saying the "Memorare" each day:

Remember O Most loving Virgin Mary, that never was it known that anyone who fled to thy protection, implored thy help or sought thy intercession, was left unaided. Inspired by this confidence I fly unto thee, O Virgin of Virgins, my mother. To thee do I come, before thee I stand, sinful and sorrowful. O Mother of the Word Incarnate, despise not my petitions, but in thy mercy, hear and answer me. Amen.

(10)

Whoever you be, Jew or Gentile, you will, on becoming a Catholic, become the spiritual seed of Abraham, the man of faith, hope and obedience, to whom the Messiah and countless seed were promised, and with the Mother of Christ (and with me) you will be able to sing the song which Mary, the Mother of God, sang after Jesus was conceived in her womb by the power of the Holy Spirit. (Luke 1:46–56):

"My soul magnifies the Lord,
    and my spirit rejoices in God my Savior;
Because he has regarded the lowliness of
    his handmaid;
For, behold, henceforth all generations shall
    call me blessed;
Because he who is mighty has done great things
    for me,
And holy is his name;
And for generation upon generation is his mercy,
    to those who fear him.
He has shown might with his arm,
    he has scattered the proud in the conceit of
      their heart.
He has put down the mighty from their thrones,
    and has exalted the lowly.

He has filled the hungry with good things.
   and the rich he has sent away empty.
He has given help to Israel, his servant,
   mindful of his mercy—
Even as he spoke to our fathers—
   to Abraham and to his posterity forever.''

AFTERWORD

THE STATE OF ISRAEL

My conversion occurred in the thirties, before the Holocaust, and before the State of Israel came into existence. I consider the Holocaust as one of the most barbarous and terrible episodes in the history of humankind. I identify with the views expressed by Archbishop Sheen regarding this nightmarish massacre given in his Preface to this book.

It seems to me that the division of Germany into two separate states, and the establishment of the State of Israel are a divine response to this terrible happening, one that is for the welfare of both the German (portending a future happy unification) and the Jewish peoples. The ultimate significance of the State of Israel must be seen, I believe, in the light of prophecy: "Now if their offense is the riches of the world, and their decline the riches of the Gentiles, how much more their full number! . . . For if the rejection of them (the Jews) is the reconciliation of the world (the Gentiles), what will the reception of them be but life from the dead?" (Romans: 11,12–15).

I see the establishment of the State of Israel as the setting of the stage for the collective conversion of the Jews prophesied by St. Paul, which will bring back to the Faith the Gentile nations who have—in large part—lost the Faith in our post-Christian era.

Yet how far away from conversion the Jewish people seem to be! But some subterranean changes may be taking place which in the moment of a great earthquake may come to the surface. Listen to an Israeli author, Professor Zweig, who published the results of a sociological study on the subject of

Jesus and the State of Israel in a book *Israel: the Sword and the Harp,* the Mystique of Violence and the Mystique of Redemption.

"The figure of Jesus, the Jew from Nazareth, looms large on the Israeli horizon, although not much is said about him openly and most Jews cautiously refrain from mentioning his name in public. Still he is very much in the mind of the Israeli Jews, more now than ever, and the awareness of his shadow in Israel is constantly growing."

"In the Galilee, the most beautiful and inspiring part of Israel, he is the dominating figure. Every site of antiquity and every beauty spot in Galilee bears his footprints. He is still walking by the sea of Galilee (Mt. 4:18), on the Sabbath day he enters the synagogue in Capernaum (Mk. 1:21), in Tabgha, close to Capernaum, he performs the miracle of the loaves and the fishes (Lk: 9:17). On the Mount of Beatitudes, which overlooks the waters of the lake, he utters his immortal Sermon on the Mount. Of course, Nazareth is the centre of his life and Jerusalem, the scene of his last ministry. Much of the charm and magnetism of the Holy Land is due, not only to echoes of the Old Testament, but also to the echoes of Jesus' life. Being confronted with Jesus in this way is a new experience for the Jew.

"In the Diaspora, Jesus looked alien to the Jew, an outsider, an interloper. But in Israel, he is seen as the Jew from Nazareth, a native of this country, a Sabra, with claims to the land as strong as any. He cannot be brushed aside as a foreign influence."

"The mystery of this simple Jew from Nazareth, who managed to conquer almost the whole world and whose spiritual power was stronger than that of the whole of Jewry is puzzling to the Israeli Jew. Who was he? Where lies the secret and mystery of his power? How did this Jew manage to attract the immense love and admiration of the whole world, while the Jews attracted only hatred and contempt? How did he manage to fulfill the task set in the Bible for the Jews, to serve as a light unto the nations, while the Jews failed miserably? Why was it that only he managed to shape and mold the world, while the Jews played a losing game, rolling in the dust? Why has the genius of Jesus never been repeated within Jewish gates? And will it be repeated?"

Professor Zweig is not a Christian. Yet he believes that the acceptance of Jesus and of his message will make "all the difference in the fight for survival by the Israeli Jews, in their development as a nation and as a spiritual force in the world, as well as for the peaceful settlement of their conflict with the Arab nations."

Perhaps even more pertinent is that Israel is seeking a mission, which it cannot find, until it receives it from the Jew from Nazareth. Then its mission will be "to bring life to the dead."

I will give two more witnesses to the change in the Jewish mentality towards Jesus as evidenced in the best of modern Jewish minds. Martin Buber said that from boyhood he had thought of Jesus as an older brother. It had been of importance to him that Christianity considered Jesus to be God and Redeemer, and he had tried to understand this. Buber believed that Jesus was a unique figure in the history of the faith of Israel.

Another outstanding Jewish thinker, the New Testament scholar Pinchas Lapide accepts the resurrection of Jesus as a reality in his recent book *The Resurrection of Jesus: A Jewish Perspective*. He recognizes in Jesus not the Messiah but a great Jewish prophet preparing the way for the messianic era, a sign of hope for Jews who are looking for the coming of the Messiah. Christianity, he believes, fulfilled the Jewish task of bringing monotheism, the God of Abraham, to the human family. Christians are the go-betweens who Judaized the pagans.

With the foundation of the Jewish state of Israel, the collective conversion of the Jews can now take place, with the survival of Jewish identity in the Jewish people, thanks to the conjunction of a land, a language, and a people.

Father Elias Friedman, a convert, and a medical doctor, who has been a member of Haifa's Carmelite monastery for twenty-five years, believes that the collective conversion of the Jews is imminent.[1] In preparation for that eventuality he has founded a Hebrew-Catholic Association. He hopes that this will become a community with its own rite within the Catholic Church. His project has the unanimous backing of the South African Bishops Conference and the support of the Apostolic Delegate of Jerusalem and is under consideration by the Vatican's Secretariat for non-Christian religions.

[1] *Jewish Identity* is an unpublished manuscript of Fr. Elias' which contains a searching analysis of the Jewish question and the role of the Jewish people in relation to Jesus and His mystical body. The quotation from Prof. Zweig's cited book is to be found in *Jewish Identity.*

Another organization interested in matters Jewish and Catholic is the Edith Stein Guild, which holds meetings and sponsors events and pilgrimages. It also publishes a Newsletter. In a recent issue, attention was called to a statement made by Pope John Paul II on his visit to Germany in 1980: "As sons and daughters of Abraham, Jews and Christians are called to be a blessing for the world. They will be a blessing if jointly they stand up for peace among all people and peoples." The editor of the Newsletter is Miss Charlotte Lowit, c/o Our Lady of Victory Church, 60 Williams St., New York, N.Y. 10005. The membership secretary is Mrs. E. Foss, 100–31 Metropolitan Avenue, Forest Hills, L.I., N.Y. 11375.

The life of Edith Stein, prominent in the women's movement in pre-World War II Germany, who met death in Auschwitz, has been recently published by Harper and Row, translated by Father Bernard Bonowitz, O.C.S.O..

NOTES

The frontispiece is a reproduction of the countenance of Jesus Christ. It is an authentic photograph of the detail of the face of the Holy Shroud, made by the official photographer.

Besides the clear Jewish features, noble, sad, majestically peaceful, this Holy Shroud carries the impression of the entire figure of Christ, with the wounds of the scourging, crowning with thorns, carrying of the cross, crucifixion, and piercing of the side with a lance. These impressions were not *distinctly* visualized until the advent of photography.

In 1898 Signor Pia, an amateur photographer, photographed the relic, and to his surprise found that his negative was a positive of the figure on the Shroud, that is, with the reversal of the light and dark impressions such as occurs in a photographic negative, a positive picture of the figure on the shroud was produced.

On May 3, 1931, the Shroud was officially rephotographed, by a recognized expert in photography, Cavalier G. Enrie. Sixteen thousand candlepower lighting was used, and many exposures were taken. This new photography vindicated and verified Signor Pia's early work.

The Gospels and the Shroud are entirely independent witnesses of the death and burial of Christ. The text of the Gospels and the impression on the relic have both been fixed in their present form, and known, for centuries; yet not until the advent of photography could the entire conformity of these two witnesses be observed. Hence they manifest the authenticity of each other as testimonies of the death of Jesus Christ.

109

The following details are recorded by the three Synoptic Evangelists, and confirmed and complemented by St. John, and are strikingly in agreement with the medico-legal evidence afforded by the Shroud. Christ was crucified and buried hastily. It was the eve of the Passover festival, Friday afternoon. There was not sufficient time to carry out the full Jewish burial ceremonies, such as the cleansing of the body, the use of an ointment for anointing the body, etc., but the holy women who accompanied Him intended to carry out these details on the following Sunday, which for the Jews was the first day of the week. A large quantity of a mixture of myrrh and aloes was used to prepare the body, and a fine linen cloth was employed to wrap it, in accordance with the burial customs of the Palestinian Jews of the time.[1] Thus St. John says:

And there also came Nicodemus (who at first had come to Jesus by night), bringing a mixture of myrrh and aloes, in weight about a hundred pounds. They therefore took the body of Jesus and wrapped it in linen cloths with the spices, after the Jewish manner of preparing for burial. Now in the place where he was crucified there was a garden, and in the garden a new tomb in which no one had yet been laid. There, accordingly, because of the Preparation Day of the Jews, for the tomb was close at hand, they laid Jesus (St. John 20:39–42).

Other details to which both Shroud and Gospels testify are these: before His death Christ was scourged and crowned with thorns by Pilate's Roman soldiers. He Himself carried His own cross. To confirm His death, before the body was delivered over to Joseph of Arimathea for burial, the centurion pierced His side with a lance, and blood issued forth.

The Shroud shows no evidence of the corruption of the body. John, who was a witness of the crucifixion, and whose testimony constitutes the fourth Gospel, attests that on the Sunday following the death of Christ, he visited the burial

[1] These matters are well presented in detail in the article, *The Shroud of Turin and the Burial of Christ*, by Rev. Edward A. Wuenschel, C.SS.R., S.T.D., in the Catholic Biblical Quarterly, April, 1946.

tomb with Peter and found the linen which had covered the body placed at one side. The holy women who had come to the tomb early that morning to complete the anointing and burial of the body had met the risen Christ, who showed them the wounds of His crucifixion as proof that it was He, and told them to return to the apostles and tell them that He had risen as He had said He would. John relates that he did not believe until, on visiting the tomb, he had inspected the linen which had covered the Body.

In October 1978 a team of forty American scientists performed thousands of scientific tests upon the Shroud. One of these scientists, Dr. John Heller, writes "The images are the result of dehydrative acid oxidation of the linen. The blood is human blood. How the images got on the cloth is a mystery." Fraud has been ruled out. Dr. Heller says that Don Lynnas "puts it well":

"It is anatomically accurate; it matches the Gospels historically; everything is correct with what we know. It is an accurate picture of the passion and death of Christ. It makes it very real that this was a man who was beaten and scourged and crucified. What you have is the Gospel, the story of Christ crucified, set forth in detail before you, to look at, appreciate and think about." See also Verdict on the Shroud, *by Kenneth E. Stevenson and Gary R. Habermas, Servant Books, Ann Arbor, Michigan, 1981. This book contains a section on the significance of the Shroud in respect to the death and resurrection of Jesus.)*

The holy Shroud then is a witness to the truth of the teaching of the Catholic Church, insofar as it is a record, which may be called the fifth Gospel, of the death, burial and resurrection of Jesus Christ. It is a confirmation of the genuineness and historical accuracy of the Gospels of Jesus Christ. As Pope Pius XI said, it presents "pictures of Christ . . . the most suggestive, most precious that one can imagine."

In the distinctly Jewish countenance which this picture presents, may be seen the bruises of Christ's Passion, including the wounds made by the crown of thorns. There is evidence of great affliction sweetly endured, and of a noble majesty. The holy Face is serene with a grief whose peace quietly manifests His triumph over death.

Certainly this is He of whom Isaiah says "He hath borne our infirmities and carried our sorrows: and we have thought Him as it were a leper, and as one struck by God and afflicted. . . . He was offered because it was His own will, and He opened not His mouth." And of whom St. John says (13.1): "Having loved His own, He loved them to the end."

NOTE ON THE SOLAR PRODIGY OF FATIMA

The great miracle of Fatima, witnessed by 70,000 people, was predicted by three children: Jacinta Marto, aged 7, Francis, her brother, aged 9, and their cousin Lucy dos Santos, aged 10, now Sister Lucy, a Carmelite. The Blessed Virgin Mary appeared to them on May 13, 1917, and asked them to return on the thirteenth of each month to the same place, the Cova da Iria, where they were accustomed to take their parents' sheep to pasture. She promised that on October 13th she would tell them who she was and what she wanted.

Much unbelief met the widespread reports of this apparition in Portugal, then in the hands of an atheistic government, hostile to the Catholic Church. (It is interesting to a Cistercian to recall that this country in which the Mother of God, Queen of Cistercians, appeared, was first recognized as an independent state through the intercession with the Holy See of the Cistercian Abbot, St. Bernard; and that its first king, Alfonso, made his dominions feudatory to Our Lady of Clairvaux, the Cistercian abbey presided over by the Saint.)

That all might believe, Mary promised a great miracle to be performed October 13, 1917. On this day 70,000 people assembled in the Cova da Iria, many during the night despite the drenching rain. These people were of all degrees of belief and unbelief, of varying education, and of all classes. Many had come merely out of curiosity to see what would happen on this day of prophecy, for it was the topic of conversation throughout Portugal.

What happened on that day will strike many as incredible; indeed many of the witnesses so described it. Learned men exclaimed, "I have seen but I cannot explain." What they saw, others within a radius of twenty-five miles likewise testified to having seen. Reporters were present and obtained photographs, and their accounts appeared in the newspapers. The director of one of the great Lisbon newspapers (Avelino d'Almeida of the *O Seculo*) had written an editorial which appeared on the morning of October 13, in which he treated the claims that the Blessed Virgin Mary, Mother of Christ, was appearing to the three shepherd children, as fraud and superstition. At noon he was present in the Cova da Iria and in the evening wrote an account of what he had witnessed, which he described as a spectacle unique and incredible for one who was not present. The Catholic Bishops of Portugal maintained an attitude of prudent reserve, as is the custom of the Church in regard to apparitions, private revelations and the like. An official ecclesiastical enquiry was instituted after five years; it lasted seven years. In 1930, the Bishop of Leiria, after many months of detailed study of the final report of this canonical Commission, pronounced the visions of the children as worthy of credence (not a matter of Catholic Faith, but worthy of belief according to all the rules of human testimony).

The incredible event witnessed by the vast multitude was preceded at noon by a flash of lightning; then Lucy, as in the previous apparitions, was heard speaking with someone to whom all three children listened with rapt attention.

After this Lucy cried out, "Oh, look at the sun!" Then for twelve minutes all witnessed the solar prodigy, which has been likened to the Old Testament miracle when at Joshua's word, as is related in Joshua 10:13, "the sun stood still." In a cloudless sky, the sun at its zenith ceased to dazzle the eye, permitting continuous direct observation without discomfort. Suddenly it began a succession of abrupt movements, and then began to revolve. It emitted great beams of light, of all colors, which extended as far as the eye could see over clouds, the earth, the people. This was witnessed in neighboring villages, and continued for about four minutes. Then the sun stopped its peculiar movements. After a few instants, these phenomena were renewed, and again after a short pause, a third time, making the facts evident beyond any doubt to all witnesses.

This was the great miracle promised by the Blessed Virgin in previous apparitions—that all those who had heard of these apparitions, and had doubted them, might believe; and that the message which she wished to convey to the world through these three children and the 70,000 witnesses might be credible in the eyes of all prudent persons. For these witnesses, in this country of Portugal, then beset by atheism and the idolatry of "progress," "science," "freedom of thought," a greater miracle was held in reserve, one which was hidden, unseen and occurred in their souls, occasioned by the last event in the solar movements. During the twelve minutes just described, the great crowd had been in suspense, breathless, immovable. Then after these gigantic supernatural fireworks, occurred an event worthy of the purposes of God, Who leads all to Himself through faith and repentance. The sun detached itself from its place in the firmament and began to fall upon the spectators. All thought the end of the world had come. With one accord, people of all classes, of all degrees of belief and unbelief, of varying education, expecting instant death, fell upon their knees, confessed their faith in God and asked pardon for their sins. This wonderful and awesome scene was suddenly terminated by the final moment of the solar prodigy. The sun stopped short in its fall, began to climb back to its place in the firmament, and resumed its natural appearance. The vast multitude departed gradually, happy, restrained, radiant, their souls bearing the imprints of a hidden miracle of grace: a rebirth of faith in God, confidence in God, contrition for their sins, and love for His adorable goodness.

The message of Fatima is a call to prayer and penance; specifically it is a call to the daily recitation of the rosary and to amendment of life. This is the message which the prophets of ancient Israel carried from God to the people. So to the new Israel, the Catholic Church, in which God treats with people now in the same fatherly way as He formerly did, He has sent his Mother.

Formerly He foretold terrible chastisements to befall an Israel which did not heed the warnings of His prophets, for example the Assyrian captivity and the Babylonian captivity, with the destruction of Jerusalem and the temple. In 1917, through Mary, He foretold a terrible war to come, famine, the destruction of nations.

God permitted Himself to be placated by the repentance of Israel, by its prayer and fasting. He confirmed His promises to it by drawing forth the promised Messiah, Jesus Christ, from Israel, from Mary, the Lily of Israel, the daughter of David. He will be placated now by the return of Christians to their Church and of the Jews to their Messiah.

On October 31st, 1942, Pius XII consecrated Russia and the whole world to the Immaculate Heart of Mary. On November 21st, 1964 Paul VI renewed this consecration. On May 13, 1982, John Paul II repeated this consecration in spiritual union with all the Bishops of the world.

On July 13, 1917, Mary said at Fatima, "If my requests are heeded, Russia will be converted and there will be peace. If not, Russia will spread her errors throughout the world, promoting wars and persecution of the Church, the good will be martyred, the Holy Father will have much to suffer, various nations will be annihilated."

Mary also made it known through Sister Lucia that the consecration God desired is a collegial consecration of the Pope together with all the Bishops of the world. And the reason for this is that devotion to the Immaculate Heart of Mary, alongside devotion to the Sacred Heart of Jesus, be established throughout the world.

In the last fifty six years, these predictions have been in the process of realization. Because the response to the requests of our Lady have been so late, particularly in regard to the condition that the Pope and the Bishops in collegial union make this consecration, a condition which does not yet seem to have been perfectly accomplished, it will undoubtedly be a correspondingly long period before her promises are fulfilled: "In the end my Immaculate heart will triumph. The Holy Father will consecrate Russia to me and she will be converted, and a period of peace will be granted to the world. In Portugal the doctrine of the Faith will always be preserved." Compare *The Sun Danced At Fatima*, Joseph Pelletier, A.A., 1983 Doubleday, N.Y., in particular Ch.23.

What the faithful acceptance of the message of Fatima—for compliance with our Lady's wishes also involves the individual and personal response of prayer and penance (i.e. fidelity to the duties of one's state of life)—can effect for the peoples of the world has been indicated at least partially in Portugal.

A brief account of the renewal of Portugal following upon the events of Fatima is given by the Reverend J. da Cruz, C.S.Sp., whose work, *Le Prodige Inoui de Fatima*, is translated by the Reverend Montes de Oca, C.S.Sp., in the little booklet *More About Fatima and the Immaculate Heart of Mary*, published in 1946.

In the Revolution of October, 1910, the "Freethinkers" had seized power with the avowed purpose of extinguishing the Faith in two generations. Within sixteen years the country had sixteen bloody revolutions, eight presidents of the Republic, and forty-three changes of ministry. The country had no longer any credit, and the League of Nations was considering placing its finances under foreign control. Together with this financial ruin went a moral ruin. Communism, organized in cells, terrorized the country. There was no longer any respect for right, justice, or public welfare. The apparitions of Fatima occurred when the country was on the point of total collapse. After the apparitions, a wonderful conversion of the people took place, commencing with the 70,000 witnesses of the solar prodigy. Within eleven years of the apparitions, a new regime of civil and religious liberty was instituted. Portugal remained untouched by World War II.

It is evident that when a people are justified within, external justice is readily established. Capable, wise, and religious men are available in every country, and when its people are worthy of just and faithful leaders, God provides them, and through them establishes order and justice. To the Jews the call of Our Lady of Fatima to repentance opens the way from a decadent society to the promised land, the Church of all nations, which God had promised to found and in which He manifestly lives and operates. All are called to confess their sinfulness and assume personal responsibility for the afflictions with which God now visits the world, the Jew as well as the Gentile. Theirs, together with all non-Catholics', is the wonderful inquiry into the question: "What think you of Christ? Who is He?" Theirs is the hope of an invincible Faith based on God's own word spoken from human lips by His divine Son, preserved by His Holy Spirit through the infallible authority of His vicar on earth, the Pope. Theirs is the hope of receiving from God, through the sacraments of His Church, which are the channels of His grace, a reborn innocence. For the sacrament of Baptism which admits the believer to all other sacraments, remits all sin. Theirs is the hope, thus admitted into the mystical Body of Christ, of being conducted by His Holy Spirit to eternal life—to Heaven, for the grace of God is the power of attaining to eternal life.

For the Jew, as for all, a new Judith has arisen to conquer their real enemies: first, the false maxims of the world, a world which does not receive the truth or walk in the way of life; secondly, the vices of the flesh which fight against the spirit and which cannot be overcome without prayer and penance; and thirdly, the wiles of Satan, who goes through the world like a raging lion seeking whom he may devour. For the Jew, as for all, a new Esther intercedes before a divine Assuerus to obtain for them entrance into the way of life and faithful perseverance in all justice, goodness, and truth. At Fatima this Protectress, who declared herself on October 13, 1917, to be Our Lady of the Rosary, opened her Immaculate Heart to all, a Heart which so loved all, that she gave her only Son for their salvation. This heart God offers as a sure ark and refuge to all those who will to be His people. In this Heart, one with the Sacred Heart of her Divine Son which wrought their salvation, people will be saved from the new deluge which threatens to submerge mankind. Through this heart they will find true and everlasting happiness in the worship of one God, God the Father, Creator of heaven and earth, God the son, Redeemer of the human race, and God the Holy Spirit, the Sanctifier, the Gift of God given at Baptism, the source of all true conversion, the divine and true Friend of the human heart, the Spirit of Love, the Dove of Peace.

APPENDIX ONE

THE CHURCH AND THE JEWS

From the "Declaration on the Relationship of the
Church to Non-Christian Religions" of Vatican Council II

4. As this Sacred Synod searches into the mystery of the
Church, it recalls the spiritual bond linking the people of the
New Covenant with Abraham's stock.

For the Church of Christ acknowledges that, according to
the mystery of God's saving design, the beginnings of her
faith and her election are already found among the patriarchs, Moses, and the prophets. She professes that all who
believe in Christ, Abraham's sons according to faith (cf. Gal.
3:7), are included in the same patriarch's call, and likewise
that the salvation of the Church was mystically foreshadowed by the chosen people's exodus from the land of
bondage.

The Church, therefore, cannot forget that she received the
revelation of the Old Testament through the people with
whom God in His inexpressible mercy deigned to establish
the Ancient Covenant. Nor can she forget that she draws
sustenance from the root of that good olive tree onto which
have been grafted the wild olive branches of the Gentiles (cf.
Rom. 11:17–24). Indeed, the Church believes that by His
cross Christ, our Peace, reconciled Jew and Gentile, making
them both one in Himself (cf. Eph. 2:14–16).

Also, the Church ever keeps in mind the words of the
Apostle about his kinsmen, "who have the adoption as sons,
and the glory and the covenant and the legislation and the
worship and the promises; who have the fathers, and from
whom is Christ according to the flesh" (Rom. 9:4–5), the son
of the Virgin Mary. The Church recalls too that from the

Jewish people sprang the apostles, her foundation stones and pillars, as well as most of the early disciples who proclaimed Christ to the world.

As Holy Scripture testifies, Jerusalem did not recognize the time of her visitation (cf.Lk. 19:44), nor did the Jews in large number accept the gospel; indeed, not a few opposed the spreading of it (cf. Rom 11:28). Nevertheless, according to the Apostle, the Jews still remain most dear to God because of their fathers, for He does not repent of the gifts He makes nor of the calls He issues (cf. Rom. 11:28–29). In company with the prophets and the same Apostle, the Church awaits that day, known to God alone, on which all peoples will address the Lord in a single voice and "serve him with one accord" (Soph. 3:9; cf. Is. 66:23; Ps. 65:4; Rom 11:11–32).

Since the spiritual patrimony common to Christians and Jews is thus so great, this sacred Synod wishes to foster and recommend that mutual understanding and respect which is the fruit above all of biblical and theological studies, and of brotherly dialogues.

True, authorities of the Jews and those who followed their lead pressed for the death of Christ (cf. Jn. 19:6); still, what happened in His passion cannot be blamed upon all the Jews then living, without distinction, nor upon the Jews of today. Although the Church is the new people of God, the Jews should not be presented as repudiated or cursed by God, as if such views followed from the holy Scriptures. All should take pains, then, lest in catechetical instruction and in the teaching of God's Word they teach anything out of harmony with the truth of the gospel and the spirit of Christ.

The Church repudiates all persecutions against any man. Moreover, mindful of her common patrimony with the Jews, and motivated by the gospel's spiritual love and by no political considerations, she deplores the hatred, persecutions, and displays of anti-Semitism directed against the Jews at any time and from any source.

Besides, as the Church has always held and continues to hold, Christ in His boundless love underwent His passion and death because of the sins of all men, so that all might attain salvation. It is, therefore, the duty of the Church's preaching to proclaim the cross of Christ as the sign of God's all-embracing love and as the fountain from which every grace flows.

5. We cannot in truthfulness call upon that God who is the Father of all if we refuse to act in a brotherly way toward certain men, created though they may be to God's image. A man's relationship with God the Father and his relationship with his brother men are so linked together that Scripture says: "He who does not love does not know God" (1 Jn. 4:8).

The ground is therefore removed from every theory or practice which leads to a distinction between men or peoples in the matter of human dignity and the rights which flow from it.

As a consequence, the Church rejects as foreign to the mind of Christ, any discrimination against men or harassment of them because of their race, color, condition of life or religion.

Documents of Vatican II, Walter Abbot, S.J., Editor, America Press, 1966.

APPENDIX TWO

THE CHURCH AND THE JEWISH BIBLE

From the "Dogmatic Constitution on Divine Revelation"
of Vatican Council II

14. In carefully planning and preparing the salvation of
the whole human race, the God of supreme love, by a special
dispensation, chose for Himself a people to whom He might
entrust his promises. First He entered into a covenant with
Abraham (cf. Gen. 15:18) and through Moses, with the
people of Israel (cf. Ex. 24:8). To this people which He had
acquired for Himself, He so manifested Himself through
words and deeds as the one true and living God that Israel
came to know by experience the ways of God with men, and
with God Himself speaking to them by the words of the
prophets, Israel daily gained a deeper and clearer understanding of His ways and made them more widely known among
the nations (Ps. 21:28–29; 95:1–3; Is. 2:1–4; Jer. 3:17). The
plan of salvation, foretold by the sacred authors, recounted
and explained by them, is found as the true word of God in the
books of the Old Testament: these books, therefore, written
under divine inspiration, remain permanently valuable.

15. . . . These same books, then, give expression to a lively
sense of God, contain a store of sublime teachings about God,
sound wisdom about human life, and a wonderful treasury of
prayers, and in them the mystery of our salvation is present
in a hidden way. Christians should receive them with
reverence.

16. God, the inspirer and author of both testaments,
wisely ordained that the New Testament be hidden in the Old

and the Old be made manifest in the New. For though Christ established the New Covenant in His blood (cf. Luke 22:20; 1 Cor. 11:25), still the books of the Old Testament with all their parts, caught up into the proclamation of the gospel, acquire and show forth their full meaning in the New Testament (cf. Mt. 5:17; Lk 24:27; Rom 1:25–26; 2 Cor. 3:14–16) and in turn shed light on it and explain it.

"Divine Revelation" Chapter 4, The Old Testament, *Documents of Vatican II,* Walter M. Abbott, S.J., editor, America Press, 1966.

APPENDIX THREE

RELIGIOUS FREEDOM and PERSECUTION

From the "Declaration on Religious Freedom"
of Vatican Council II

1. . . . First, this sacred Synod professes its belief that God himself has made known to mankind the way in which men are to serve Him, and thus be saved in Christ and come to blessedness. We believe that this one true religion subsists in the Catholic and apostolic Church, to which the Lord Jesus committed the duty of spreading it abroad among all men . . . On their part, all men are bound to seek the truth, especially in what concerns God and His Church, and to embrace the truth they come to know, and to hold fast to it. This sacred Synod likewise professes its belief that it is upon the human conscience that these obligations fall and exert their binding force. The truth cannot impose itself except by virtue of its own truth, as it makes its entrance into the mind at once quietly and with power. Religious freedom, in turn, which men demand as necessary to fulfill their duty to worship God, has to do with immunity from coercion in civil society . . .

2. This Vatican Synod declares that the human person has a right to religious freedom. This freedom means that all men are to be immune from coercion on the part of individuals and social groups and of any human power, in such wise that in matters religious no one is to be forced to act in a manner contrary to his own beliefs. Nor is anyone to be restrained from acting in accordance with his own beliefs, whether privately or publicly, whether alone or in association with others, within due limits . . .

They (men and women) are also bound to adhere to the truth, once it is known, and to order their whole lives in accord with the demands of truth.

However, men cannot discharge these obligations in a manner in keeping with their own nature unless they enjoy immunity from external coercion as well as psychological freedom. Therefore, the right to religious freedom has its foundation, not in the subjective disposition of the person, but in his very nature. In consequence, the right to this immunity continues to exist even in those who do not live up to their obligation of seeking the truth and adhering to it . . .

3. . . . Truth, however, is to be sought after in a manner proper to the dignity of the human person and his social nature . . . In all his activity a man is bound to follow his conscience faithfully, in order that he may come to God, for whom he was created . . .

For, of its very nature, the exercise of religion consists before all else in those internal, voluntary, and free acts whereby man sets the course of his life directly toward God. No merely human power can either command or prohibit acts of this kind.

However, the social nature of man itself requires that he should give external expression to his internal acts of religion; that he should participate with others in matters religious; that he should profess his religion in community. Injury, therefore, is done to the human person and to the very order established by God for human life, if the free exercise of religion is denied in society when the just requirements of public order do not so require . . .

Government therefore ought indeed to take account of the religious life of the people and show it favor, since the function of government is to make provision for the common welfare. However, it would clearly transgress the limits set to its power were it to presume to direct or inhibit acts that are religious.

4. . . . Religious bodies also have the right not to be hindered in their public teaching and witness to their faith, whether by the spoken or by the written word. However, in spreading religious faith and in introducing religious practices, everyone ought at all times to refrain from any manner of action which might seem to carry a hint of coercion or of a kind of persuasion that would be dishonorable or unworthy, especially when dealing with poor or uneducated people. Such a manner of action would have to be considered an abuse of one's own right and a violation of the right of others . . .

5. Since the family is a society in its own original right, it has the right freely to live its own domestic religious life under the guidance of parents. Parents, moreover, have the right to determine, in accordance with their own religious beliefs, the kind of religious education that their children are to receive.

Government, in consequence, must acknowledge the right of parents to make a genuinely free choice of schools and of other means of education. The use of this freedom of choice is not to be made a reason for imposing unjust burdens on parents, whether directly or indirectly. Besides, the rights of parents are violated if their children are forced to attend lessons or instruction which are not in agreement with their religious beliefs. The same is true if a single system of education, from which all religious formation is excluded, is imposed upon all.

6. . . . Government is also to help create conditions favorable to the fostering of religious life, in order that the people may be truly enabled to exercise their religious rights and to fulfill their religious duties, and also in order that society itself may profit by the moral qualities of justice and peace which have their origin in men's faithfulness to God and to His holy will.

. . . finally, government is to see to it that the equality of citizens before the law, which is itself an element of the common welfare, is never violated for religious reasons whether openly or covertly. Nor is there to be discrimination among citizens . . .

7. . . . Men are to deal with their fellows in justice and civility.

. . . For the rest, the usages of society are to be the usages of freedom in their full range. These require that the freedom of man be respected as far as possible, and be curtailed only when and insofar as necessary.

8. . . . On the other hand, not a few can be found who seem inclined to use of freedom as the pretext for refusing to submit to authority and for making light of the duty of obedience.

Therefore, this Vatican Synod urges everyone, especially those who are charged with the task of educating others, to do their utmost to form men who will respect the moral order and be obedient to lawful authority. Let them form men too who will be lovers of true freedom—men, in other words, who will come to decisions on their own judgment and in the light of truth, govern their activities with a sense of responsibility, and strive after what is true and right, willing always to join with others in cooperative effort . . .

9. . . . Revelation . . . gives evidence of the respect which Christ showed toward the freedom with which man is to fulfill his duty of belief in the Word of God. It gives us lessons too in the spirit which disciples of such a Master ought to make their own and to follow in every situation . . .

10. It is one of the major tenets of Catholic doctrine that man's response to God in faith must be free. Therefore no one is to be forced to embrace the Christian faith against his own will . . . The act of faith is of its very nature a free act. Man, redeemed by Christ the Savior, and through Christ

Jesus called to be God's adopted son, cannot give his adherence to God revealing Himself unless the Father draw him to offer to God the reasonable and free submission of faith.

It is therefore completely in accord with the nature of faith that in matters religious every manner of coercion on the part of men should be excluded . . .

11. . . . Taught by the word and example of Christ, the apostles followed the same way. From the very origins of the Church the disciples of Christ strove to convert men to faith in Christ as the Lord—not, however, by the use of coercion or by devices unworthy of the gospel, but by the power, above all, of the Word of God . . .

12. The Church therefore is being faithful to the truth of the gospel, and is following the way of Christ and the apostles when she recognizes, and gives support to, the principle of religious freedom as befitting the dignity of man and as being in accord with divine revelation . . . In the life of the People of God as it has made its pilgrim way through the vicissitudes of human history, there have at times appeared ways of acting which were less in accord with the spirit of the gospel and even opposed to it. Nevertheless, the doctrine of the Church that no one is to be coerced into faith has always stood firm . . .

14. . . . The disciple is bound by a grave obligation toward Christ his Master ever more adequately to understand the truth received from Him, faithfully to proclaim it, and vigorously to defend it, never—be it understood—having recourse to means that are incompatible with the spirit of the gospel. At the same time, the charity of Christ urges him to act lovingly, prudently and patiently in his dealings with those who are in error or in ignorance with regard to the faith. All is to be taken into account—the Christian duty to Christ, the lifegiving Word which must be proclaimed, the rights of the human person, and the measure of grace

granted by God through Christ to men, who are invited freely to accept and profess the faith.

15. . . . Consequently, in order that relationships of peace and harmony may be established and maintained within the whole of mankind, it is necessary that religious freedom be everywhere provided with an effective constitutional guarantee, and that respect be shown for the high duty and right of man freely to lead his religious life in society.

The Documents of Vatican II, Walter Abbot, S.J., editor, America Press, 1966.

ANALYTICAL TABLE OF CONTENTS
A Summary

CHAPTER ONE: GOD IS NO LONGER IN THE MIDST OF HIS PEOPLE

(1) Resolved: never to abandon the Jewish religion; by becoming a Catholic this resolution is kept.
(2) The orthodox Jewish religion.
(3) Public High School: anti-Church, anti-religion; one teacher speaks in favor of God.

CHAPTER TWO: SEARCH FOR THE KINGDOM OF TRUTH

(1) At the University of Michigan: discovery of the want of unity in modern education.
(2) At the University of Berlin: glimpses of the secret Kingdom of Truth.
(3) Friends on the way to the goal.
(4) At Medical School: Aristotelian Philosophy, St. Thomas Aquinas and the changeless Truth: what is wanting in modern education is the knowledge of true philosophy.
(5) At the University of Chicago: Dr. Robert Maynard Hutchins takes the lead in modern education by introducing into it the knowledge of true philosophy.
(6) Logic and Metaphysics: the existence of truth, the knowledge of natural principles.
(7) Doubts concerning evolution: failure of the attempt to explain creation without admitting a Creator.
(8) Origin of the human race: not from apes but from first human parents.
(9) Immaterial ideas require an immaterial power of reason, an immaterial and hence incorruptible soul.
(10) The Angels: complete immaterial intelligent beings.
(11) The Five Proofs of the Existence of God.
(12) Aristotle's wisdom, knowledge, science and logic; his devotion to truth. St. Thomas' perfect understanding of and agreement with the philosophy of Aristotle; his similar devotion to truth; his application of the philosophic method to the examination of the revealed truths of the

131

Catholic religion. I can no longer despise the Catholic Faith nor refuse to examine it.

(13) The Infallible Teaching Authority of the Catholic Church; the logical invulnerability of its Faith: all its doctrine must be divinely true if any if it is divinely true; for it is proposed on God's authority, on God's Word.

(14) Moral values are real; the Ten Commandments express the natural moral law.

(15) Human Happiness cannot be found in creatures, but only in God; virtue is the power of attaining Happiness; grace is the gift of this power.

(16) Discovery of the insufficiency of philosophy and natural means for achieving Happiness: the Gap.

(17) God bridges the Gap for me. "Oh you of little faith."

CHAPTER THREE: GOD'S KINGDOM: FRIENDSHIP WITH GOD THROUGH FAITH IN THE GODHEAD OF JESUS CHRIST

(1) God takes me up the spiritual mountain.

(2) The Name of Jesus.

(3) The Gospel of Jesus Christ; "Who do you say that I am?"

(4) My question is likewise answered; His authority is from God, His Father; He is true God.

(5) The Resurrection of Jesus Christ; He passes through the locked door of my heart—I believe in the Godhead of Jesus Christ.

(6) "How sweet is the Lord": the gentleness and lovableness of Jesus; His Revelation is the revelation and sharing of the interior life of God.

(7) His merciful kindness: the gratuitousness of the gift of Faith and of the friendship of God.

(8) The Blessed Trinity; the Word made Flesh is come to win the friendship of men. I saw His glory, the glory of the Only-Begotten of the Father, full of grace and truth.

(9) The life of union with God: God dwells in the heart of the true believer. The validity of Catholic moral principles; the peace of a good conscience.

(10) I determine to be baptized in the Holy Roman Catholic Church.

CHAPTER FOUR: GOD'S KINGDOM: JESUS CHRIST AND THE ROMAN CATHOLIC CHURCH—ONE BODY

(1) Traveling in Europe-"Blessed are the poor in spirit."

(2) Traveling to the kingly city of God.

(3) Our first parents; Adam and Eve; the Fall.

(4) Its consequences: explanation of evil.

(5) The Redeemer comes.

(6) The Particular and Final Judgments.

(7) Mankind without a covenant, and under the old Covenant; the New Covenant: the Catholic Church is the Kingdom of God: Triumphant—in Heaven, Militant—on earth.

(8) The greatness of the Jewish race is extolled by Catholic doctrine.

(9) The way to the heavenly city; I prepare for Baptism—incorporation into the Mystical Body of Christ—the Church; divine character of the Church.

(10) Justice comes not through Communism, but through Christ. The ideal of Communism is anarchy: an impossible society, without God. The way of Communism is perpetual bloody revolution—the extermination of men. The ideal of the Church is Jesus Christ. The Way is Baptism which requires faith in the Divinity of Christ and renunciation of internal disorder—the extermination of sin. Justice—the justification of the internal as well as of external life—comes through Jesus Christ.

CHAPTER FIVE: FULFILLMENT: GOD DWELLS WITH THE SPIRITUAL DESCENDANTS OF THE JEWS

(1) In the Catholic Church I find God dwelling in the midst of His people, the spiritual descendants of the Jews.

(2) God's signature is on this Church: the miracles He works in it.

(3) The Church is holy: Her activity on behalf of men and women.

(4) My life in the Church: all my desires are fulfilled.

(5) In the Church: my external life: psychiatry, family, friends.

(6) In the Church: culmination in the religious life; the perfect Christian life. Reality of Jesus Christ. Perfect union with Jesus, the ideal of the religious life, is not a delusion: proof from the visible achievements of contemplatives.

(7) Source of true life is the life of prayer. Mary the Mother of Jesus and our Mother: a source of the knowledge of Jesus, and of the Cross of Christ. The holy Rosary and its Mysteries.

(8) The Holy Spirit and his preaching of the Word of God is the Source of true and everlasting life and of the life of prayer. His preaching to and about the Jews through St. Peter and St. Paul. "The gifts and the call of God (to the Jews, to be His people) are without repentance."

(9) The glorification of the Blessed Virgin Mary, Mother of God, Mother of fair love, Mother of grace. Her charming motherly lowliness.

(10) Holy Mary's "Magnificat," and mine, and yours if you will: "He has given help to Israel, his servant, mindful of His mercy—even as He spoke to our fathers—to Abraham and to his posterity forever."